To the
N.A. Taylor Foundation,
with thanks for
your support of
World Wildlife Fund.

Jan/02.

Wintergreen

Wintergreen

REFLECTIONS

FROM LOON LAKE

Monte Hummel

KEY PORTER BOOKS

Canadian Cataloguing in Publication Data

Hummel, Monte, 1947–
    Wintergreen

ISBN 1-55263-049-8

1. Natural history — Ontario — Loon Lake Region (Frontenac). 2. Outdoor life — Ontario — Loon Lake Region (Frontenac). 3. Hummel, Monte, 1947– . I. Title.

QH106.205H85 1999	508.713'71	C99-931326-6

Henderson Book Series No. 28

The Henderson Book Series honours the kind and generous donation of Mrs. Arthur T. Henderson, who made this series possible. The Canadian Parks and Wilderness Society gratefully acknowledges Mrs. Henderson's support of our efforts to build public support for protecting Canada's wilderness areas.

THE CANADA COUNCIL | LE CONSEIL DES ARTS
FOR THE ARTS | DU CANADA
SINCE 1957 | DEPUIS 1957

The publisher gratefully acknowledges the support of the Canada Council for the Arts and the Ontario Arts Council for its publishing program.

Canadä

We acknowledge the financial support of the Government of Canada through the Book Publishing Industry Development Program (BPIDP) for our publishing activities.

Key Porter Books Limited
70 The Esplanade
Toronto, Ontario
Canada M5E 1R2

www.keyporter.com

Design: Peter Maher
Illustrations: Dorothy Siemens
Electronic formatting: Heidy Lawrance Associates
Typeset in Fournier and Voluta Script
Printed and bound in Canada
Printed on 100% acid-free recycled paper

99 00 01 02 03 6 5 4 3 2 1

Contents

Summer

Fall

To Evan Jack,
who taught me the lay of the land "up country,"
how to prune a pine, and
where to cast for bass in Loon Lake.
In November 1996,
I named the property we both loved so much
Evan's Woods on the first anniversary of his death,
and I have protected it in his memory for 999 years
through a Conservation Agreement with the
Nature Conservancy of Canada.
Someday, my friend,
we'll walk your woods together again.

Acknowledgements

MOST OF THIS BOOK was handwritten in my cabin by
Loon Lake, some of it by candlelight. To produce it, I have
drawn on both practical and spiritual experience, as well as
the natural and human history of the area.

First, I am indebted to a foundation, wishing to remain
anonymous, whose representative simply said, "Monte, we
want to help with a project of personal interest to *you*."
Now that I have finished, my fear is that it will be of
personal interest *only* to me!

Thank you also to Francis Walker, my neighbor and
friend some distance away, who along with his father, Archie,
before him has kindly kept an eye on the cabin when I'm not
there, towed us by tractor out of mud and snow, helped me
split wood for the winter, and straightened this forester out
on what a whiffletree is.

I thank James Duncan with the Nature Conservancy of
Canada, as well as my longtime personal friend and lawyer,
Harry Wylde, for their professional counsel in preparing a
Conservation Agreement for Evan's Woods. If nothing else,
I hope this book serves to encourage other Canadians who
enjoy the privilege of being landowners to be landstewards,
and to extend that stewardship beyond your lifetime.

I would also like to thank Mary Jack for her continuing
friendship and interest in what happens to her late husband's
beloved "up country."

Thank you, Stan Rowe, Kevin Kavanagh, and Ann Love,
for providing valued comments on my manuscript in draft
form. You were chosen, because I *do* value your judgment.

Thank you, Anna Porter, Publisher of Key Porter Books, for your own commitment to conservation in Canada. Thanks also to Laurie Coulter, who has now reviewed no fewer than four of my books published under the Key Porter banner, and to Patrick Crean and Doris Cowan, my helpful editors on this one.

Finally, thank you, Sherry, my wife and loving kindred spirit, who almost alone understands what wild places mean to me, especially Loon Lake. Thanks for word-processing my handwritten manuscripts, for enduring the many edits, for providing improvements of your own, and for being the kind of person who still marvels at what others don't even notice.

Introduction

THIS BOOK IS ABOUT GETTING to know a place so
well that it becomes part of you. The boundary between self
and place dissolves. Some kind of life force or shared blood
supply flows evenly through you both without the slightest
hesitation. You feel entirely and deeply comfortable saying
"I am *of* this place; I *am* this place." Aldo Leopold, the
author of *A Sand County Almanac*, described it as "fitting
into the landscape."

In my experience, virtually anyone who has lived for a
time on the land, especially alone, instinctively knows what
I'm trying to express here. But this feeling of being one
with a "home place" is not reserved for hermits, mystics,
and poets. Nor is it a function of privilege or ability to
travel. Maybe it's where you were raised as a child. Maybe
it's a cottage, a camp, or some revisited retreat discovered
on a holiday. Maybe it's a wild isolated place, or a small city
park, or a remnant ravine that you just know you know
better than anyone else. Or maybe it's where you live and
work every day, on a farm, in the woods, or out on the
water. For many Aboriginal people it is a deep, direct union
with the land itself, something that is not often experienced
or easily understood by an increasingly urban society.

Wherever this place may be, it's a safe harbor that makes
no unwelcome demands. It serves as a source of sanity when
everything else seems to be flying apart. It is not an escape
from reality, but a return to what really counts and what
counts as real. When we find this place, we know it without

question when we are there, it is with us even when we are
not there, and we yearn to return to it in the end.

In my case, the place I have come to know better than
any other is 270 acres (110 ha) surrounding a remote cabin
nestled in the bush on the shore of a small lake on the
Canadian Shield northwest of Kingston, Ontario. More than
anything else, this place has been an enduring sanctuary for
me from a very demanding work schedule, and a spiritual
wellspring that reminds me why I do what I do.

For years now, my habit (and firm resolve) has been to
be in my cabin for a few days every month, longer in the
spring and fall. In order to ensure that these stays actually
happen, they must be scheduled weeks and often months in
advance. Although I am mainly alone, my family knows
they are welcome to join me, and they often do. But they
also know that Loon Lake is where I will be, no matter what.
My great regret, after thirty years of full-time involvement
in the Canadian and world conservation movement, is that
I have not taken more time to experience what we have all
worked so hard to protect. Because without dipping back
into our source regularly, any of us can lose our way.

Loon Lake is a half-mile (1 km) gouge sculpted by
glaciers more than ten thousand years ago from ancient
Precambrian bedrock. The land was subsequently carpeted
by a mixed forest that has evolved primarily in the hands
of natural forces such as fire, flood, disease, windthrow,
decomposition, and regeneration, resulting in a rough mosaic
of beaver ponds, marshes, rocky ridges, and woodlands—all
rich in wildlife. My cabin has no hydroelectric power, no
running water (which must instead be fetched in pails from

the lake), no telephone, cellphone, fax or electronic mail. A shortwave radio, along with my own experience of the wind and skies, brings me weather forecasts. My cabin is heated simply by a cast-iron woodburning stove. If this were an inn, I'd charge extra for all this lack of "luxury," because with a little skill a person can be comfortably dry, warm, and entirely well provided for here during any season.

I have been able to take some simple steps to extend legal protection of my piece of Canada beyond my lifetime, for no less than 999 years! Such steps are relatively new, but available right now to anyone in Canada, without relinquishing private ownership, if that is your wish. This arrangement has given me great peace of mind, because to harm a place such as Evan's Woods on Loon Lake would be unthinkable. Instead, I can go to my grave knowing that I have done something long-lasting and irrevocable to leave one small part of the Earth as I found it.

The cold facts are these: if we are to protect the ecological tapestry of Canada, then private individuals will have to play their part in the approximately one-third of our natural regions where a significant portion of the land is privately owned. With about half of the country's endangered, threatened and vulnerable wildlife species occurring on private land, such action is crucial to their future. Indeed, if the human species could expand our individual experiences of special places to collectively regard our entire planet as a cherished natural home place, it would do much to safeguard all life on Earth.

Ironically, the clues to deepening our concern for the larger world are immediately before our eyes, and easily accessible

by anyone. We need look no further than the simplest things
in Nature: cheerful mouse tracks in the snow on a woodpile;
the first brave spring peeper to speak up at dusk in April; a
quiet heron, still-fishing in a sultry summer bay; the fragrance
of fallen leaves brewing in fresh rain on the forest floor in
October; or a small wintergreen plant thriving year-round
under pines on a point jutting out into Loon Lake.

These, along with infinitely more in the supporting cast,
are bit players in the theater of evolution, which stages
magnificent annual productions regardless of what humans
consider to be important; regardless, for that matter, of
whether we even pay attention to the show. Nature's players
take their cues from the lead role played by the seasons.
Largely unnoticed, quite capable of playing their parts
without human interest, these simple things offer us nothing
less than a glimpse of the eternal.

What follows are snippets of experiences accounting
for what Loon Lake and its ecological players have come to
mean to me, accompanied by reflections on what they might
mean to all of us. I hope these thoughts resonate with how
you feel about an important place in your life.

Winter

Stepping Inside

Woodfires, Woodpiles, Woodstoves, and Woodsmoke

Dancing Shadows

Night Travel, Tea, and Bannock

Howling for Wolves

Winter Storm

Snowlife

Winter Birds

Orion's Sky

Walking on Water

Steaming Horses

Rest

Stepping Inside

IT'S A QUARTER-MILE (0.5 KM) snowshoe trip from a plowed road to my cabin, over fresh, clean snow. I pull my supplies in on a toboggan, lashed and packed according to a "system" that has proven itself over the years. When I arrive, no matter how much snow I knock off my boots before opening the cabin door, there's always enough left to deserve one more good "stomp!" on the first step inside. That footfall, sending bits of snow packed by my boot treads scuttling across the floor, is the only human sound to resonate in my cabin now for a month or so. And it feels like it.

Anyone stepping inside a small building that has been left alone for a while in midwinter knows that cold-muffled sound. On the one hand, you're aware of breaking a long-held silence; on the other hand, you're introducing the cheerful spirit of new activity.

Inside my cabin the cold-set wood rafters, walls, and floors creak, the pots and pans jiggle, and the steel stovepipe rattles as I slip across a dry floor on wet boots to open things up and start a fire in the woodstove. Opening the stove door produces the squealing tune of cold cast iron against cold cast iron, further breaking winter's spell. I scrape out my last stay's ashes with a small shovel perfectly made for the job. Next comes the rustling of dry newspaper, the snapping and laying of kindling, the thud of small logs piled in waiting by the stove, then the scratch and flare of a stick match. The stove door closes with a loud clank. Stove and chimney drafts are adjusted with a squeak. The fire takes off with a crackle and spit. Cold still air that has settled down the chimney is driven out with a roar as the fire feeds on its fresh new air supply. The warming stovepipe starts "ticking," now more rapidly and loudly, as the whole unit pours welcome heat into the one-room cabin. Before long, I can't see my breath anymore!

Outside, a young red squirrel in an old red oak philosophically takes in the entire production, including all the shuffling and bumping inside. The squirrel's observation? "Humans can't seem to do much without making noise."

Perhaps that is how we will be collectively remembered.

Wood fires, Woodpiles, Woodstoves, and Woodsmoke

WOOD FIRES

I know a fire ecologist who proudly renders fire down to two words: "rapid oxidization." Well, maybe. But that doesn't really do justice to fire as it has been experienced in the everyday lives of people. What *is* it about flames in a campfire or a fireplace that inexplicably holds our gaze and sets us thinking?

Perhaps it's because fire is primal. It was consistently put forward by pre-Socratic and Greek philosophers as one of a handful of irreducible elements that account for there being something rather than nothing.

Perhaps it's because fire has shaped nearly every landscape settled by humans, certainly in North America. In effect, we have plunked our campsites, farms, towns, and cities down into what Nature has treated for millennia as "fuel." Communities as far away from each other as those in the subarctic boreal forest of the Yukon and those in the southwestern chaparral of California are still reminded of this raw fact every year during Nature's fire seasons. Odd that everything from pine trees to prairies has adapted to this recurring natural force, indeed depends on it, yet fire is so often regarded as a "threat" by people.

On the other hand, we humans have traditionally used fire to drive game, clear land, wage war, and incinerate what we don't want ("rapid decomposition"). It has provided necessary heat for warmth and cooking, both inside and outside our dwellings, and the hearth still serves as a natural gathering place for home and family.

Wood fires are in effect the release of heat from material built up through the miraculous process of photosynthesis. This process, translated literally as "making from light," accounts for the global green contract with plants that provides all the free oxygen we breathe, in exchange for carbon. Photosynthesis is driven by the Sun, the ultimate energy-source for almost all life on Earth. Therefore, you can rightly think of that nice wood fire in winter as the brave flicker of Life itself—a thought deep enough to transfix anyone. Furthermore, it is your chance to reach back and re-experience the same heat you felt over the last few summers!

WOODPILES

At Loon Lake, the energy from past summers is stored in the cellulose rings of standing trees, some of which die; are further dried out by the Sun; then find their way, cut into stove-lengths, to my woodpile. In effect, a woodpile transfers yesterday's energy to today. The little mouse whose tracks tickle the snow on my woodpile, and whose nest is safely sheltered deep inside, little knows that it would perish instantly if the Sun's heat stored in those logs were released all at once.

My woodpile, of course, gets transformed into usable heat inside my woodstove. But on the way, I have a chance to learn more precisely about past summers by examining the width of growth rings on the logs. That thick layer laid down in 1996 in the oak log, now in my hand, corresponds nicely with the extra growth between whorls on my white pines still living in the forest: a wet summer meant good growth for oaks that year, and for pines a year later since their growth is preformed in the buds a year in advance. Counting back on the oak, I see a series of narrow rings representing the summers of 1989–92, when gypsy moths defoliated virtually all the oaks in my area. Fewer leaves meant fewer little photosynthetic factories to help build cellulose on oak trunks and branches. But you would never know that from the pines, which were untouched by the gypsy moth and instead grew faster in the extra sunlight they enjoyed when surrounding oaks lost their leaves. A bad year for oaks can be a good one for pines. The score was evened later, however, when blister rust and shoot weevil invaded my pines, but left the oaks unscathed.

And so it goes. Fits and starts are distributed unevenly across species by the even hand of Nature. As a result, growth rings in a log cross-section can be read right back to the big fire at the turn of the century which marked the birth of many of my trees, and well past that for the fire-scarred old-timers that predated and survived the blaze. There's a history of the township in this log, and I'm about to burn the book.

But before I actually load any log into the stove, there are a few more matters to weigh. First, the tree species. Is this a piece of poplar, pine, oak, or maple? The first two provide quick, short-lived heat; the others burn evenly and longer. How heavy is it? The heavy ones are not completely dried yet, and moisture content really slows burning, so that even the best firewood species won't burn well when wet. How about size and shape? Big wood is usually split, providing irregular edges that help with stacking in the stove and getting air around the log for efficient burning. Round logs are okay, but generally better if they're small or stacked on top of others in the fire. Do I want coals to cook on? If so, how soon? Am I heating water on the stovetop? For use now or later? Am I going out for a long walk and unconcerned about whether the fire goes out? Or do I want to come back to a warm cabin? Or maybe I'm laying in an all-nighter when it's forty below, in which case I *really* don't want the fire to go out. These are all calculations made in about the time it takes to reach for a log and either set it aside for later or toss it in.

WOODSTOVES

Its moods might as well be your own, because every woodstove behaves differently. But once you figure it out through trial and error, you have a well-understood companion for life. One of the wisest things anyone can do in operating a woodstove is to consult with the person who has lived with it and knows what it likes. This simple piece of advice will save you a lot of learning and a cold night.

My particular stove is a Favorite Box 25, a model made in a small town cross-country called Carleton Place, once famous in Ontario for its manufacture of good-quality cast-iron stoves. Over the years, stoves cast in Carleton Place found their way into thousands of homes, cottages, cabins, and remote camps throughout the North, often transported by horse-drawn sleighs in the early days as the heaviest single item inside, but deeply appreciated once arrived. My own little stove probably weighs 250 pounds (114 kg), so I, too, am glad it is already set in place. It stands ready to provide reliable heat and comfort for generations of people, heat borrowed from generations of trees—a nice example of living off Nature's interest rather than her capital.

W OODSMOKE

To turn a phrase, "Where there's fire, there's smoke." And there are times when you want to experience the sweet smell of woodsmoke, other times when you don't. Just about any time outdoors I do, just about any time indoors I don't, especially in winter.

For example, there's the reassuring, cozy smell of woodsmoke coming from the chimney of my cabin, wafted downwind when I'm outside fetching wood or water. It reminds me that I'm settled in and comfortable, much as I imagine others must be when I approach their place and see woodsmoke curling from the chimney. It is a Christmas-card kind of image, I suppose, but it nevertheless appeals to something elemental in human nature, especially when you are responsible for your own warmth and survival in subzero temperatures.

Then there's the smell of woodsmoke from an open fire outdoors in winter. On some occasions, for instance when warming others or myself after falling through the ice, I have welcomed this smell as a lifesaver. Also, when you are winter camping and sleeping out under the stars, a good reflector fire does more than simply "add to the atmosphere"; it is essential for survival. But usually a fire outdoors in winter, by night or day, is not an urgent matter. It is informally thrown together with small wood, to heat a quick cup of tea, cook bannock, dry out mitt-liners, or just sit beside. And if you've chosen a sheltered-enough spot, woodsmoke inevitably demonstrates its time-honored ability to find you, no matter where you sit around the fire.

My moosehide mitts smell of woodsmoke because they were smoke-tanned by the Gwich'in people of Old Crow in the Yukon. But by the time I return from an extended winter trip in the bush at Loon Lake, the rest of me smells smoke-tanned as well. Truth be known, it's nice to dig out my mitts in June, to recall these wood-smoked moments of winter.

Dancing Shadows

... I SURFACE FROM A DEEP sleep, wrapped in a six-point Hudson's Bay blanket. It's thirty below outside my cabin, and as still and clear as a winter night can be in January. The shifting, heavy ice on Loon Lake groans loudly, and Venus gleams bright blue through my east window. With one drowsy eye, I see dancing shadows on the cabin wall, flickering reflections of the fire that crackles quietly in my woodstove. ...

... I surface from a deep sleep, wrapped in an eiderdown sleeping bag, on a crinkly waterproof tarp on the snow. In front of me is a reassuring night-fire, burning now yellow, now orange, now blue, on a thick base of glowing red coals. The fire is backed by four horizontally stacked logs to reflect the heat back into my outdoor lean-to of fresh-cut poles and a bed of balsam boughs. With one drowsy eye, I see dancing shadows on the reflecting logs, and watch a spark glide up to join the stars. ...

... I surface from a deep sleep, wrapped in an eiderdown bag, on a stiff groundsheet in my snowhouse. This one was carefully hollowed out of a snow heap, mounded by using one of my snowshoes as a shovel earlier in the afternoon. By now the flickering candle burning inside, along with my breath, has glazed the ceiling that reflects dancing shadows in my cozy winter burrow. Outside, Orion brandishes his sword to chase Taurus westward before dawn. ...

... I surface from a deep sleep in my tent, slip on my boots, and step outside into the snow and darkness to behold the aurora borealis. Dancing shadows of pale green fluidly shift and inject soft neon hues up into the starlit dome overhead. If the northern lights are this breathtaking now, what have I missed while I slept? And what will I miss by going back inside? ...

These are dancing shadows of the North, witnessed by generations of our kind, back to the First Peoples. To experience them you must slip into ancient night rhythms that last as long as your campfire burns, then restoke, and lapse back into dreams permeated by the night spirits moving all around you. Ask a trapper who has spent weeks on the trail in winter. He'll tell you he never slept better in his life.

Night Travel, Tea, and Bannock

NIGHT TRAVEL

In biologists' terms, people are diurnal beings. This means we have become accustomed to venturing outdoors and living our lives primarily by day, while sleeping at night. Consequently, our night knowledge of Nature is very limited. Too bad, because we miss experiencing the natural world at a time when an abundance of nocturnal beings find it absolutely the best time to be out and about. Then, everything from spiders to coyotes can be readily identified using eyeshine reflected back from a hand-held flashlight. One keen night naturalist I know uses a miner's lamp mounted on his forehead for this purpose, directing the beam flawlessly while keeping both hands free!

In fact, we humans have quite good night vision if we simply remove ourselves from artificial light long enough to allow our eyes to become dark-adapted. But by far the nicest time to travel at night is in midwinter, using moonlight and snowshoes to get around. On a bright night, tiny snow-diamonds show themselves scattered between moon shadows.

But even without a moon, snow reflects a surprising amount of soft night light, illuminating a natural night world every bit as wonderful as our more accustomed day-lit universe.

TEA

Crossing Loon Lake, and then up to the beaver ponds that feed it, I stop in the lee of a deadfall to build a quick fire. First, I gather papery birch bark and dry firewood broken off standing drowned timber. Next, I clear snow from a spot down to the ground for the fire, and set up two side-by-side rocks, trapper style, to hold my small teapot over the flames. Then, with a match waterproofed by dipping the head in paraffin wax, the birch bark as tinder, and fine branches for kindling, my fire is born and takes off.

The best tea is brewed from melted snow in a forty-eight-ounce juice can with a snare wire handle, preferably blackened on the outside from frequent use and cached in the bush for just such a night. Second best is using a trusty small billy-pot you pack in yourself, with a tea bag fetched from your pocket. And a distant third is sipping preheated tea from the lid-cup of a stainless-steel thermos.

BANNOCK

Bannock is best made from water and biscuit dough mixed to a consistency such that it can be shaped around the blunt end of a stick. It is cooked to a golden brown by turning the stick-end slowly over a steady fire, then pulling the bannock off in one piece so that the hole can be filled with jam. Second best is frying or baking the dough in a pan, a favorite of Aboriginal peoples throughout the North. And a distant third is packing in pre-made biscuits, wrapped in foil, to be reheated in campfire coals.

TEA AND BANNOCK

Tea and bannock are best enjoyed together, outdoors under the stars by a fire, sitting on one snowshoe laid flat as a seat, and leaning up against the other jabbed tail-first into the snow as a chairback. There are really are no other choices worth mentioning.

Howling for Wolves

SNOWSHOEING AT NIGHT provides the best chance to howl for wolves or coyotes. This is now a proven technique for locating and censusing wild canids, pioneered and taught to me by the late Douglas Pimlott in the course of his wolf research in Algonquin Park. The morning of my first day on the job with World Wildlife Fund in 1978 was spent delivering the eulogy at Doug's memorial service, at his request before he died of cancer. We played tape-recorded wolf howls from happier days in the field as a tribute to his work—a powerful and emotional way for me to begin in my new position.

The general idea is pretty simple: make a convincing howl like a wolf and the wolf calls back. Those of us who do this like to pretend it takes years of experience and hard-earned woodlore. The truth is that almost anyone can make the most amateurish wolflike sound, and if the wolves are nearby and in the mood, they will likely respond. Only the occasional timber wolf makes its way down to Loon Lake, though coyotes (known locally as "brush wolves") are resident and just as responsive to human howls.

There are a few important catches, however. Things work best by far at night, when there is little wind, and at times other than when pups are expected or newly born. In fact, humans howling near active dens or rendezvous sites in the spring can be very intrusive and cause wolves to move out; during this season it is probably better to simply enjoy spontaneous howls than to try to stimulate them. Finally, human noise, including coughing and talking, should be kept to an absolute minimum. Snowshoeing on a quiet night in midwinter nicely meets all of these requirements.

I stop on a ridge long enough to allow silence to wash out the rhythmic sound of my snowshoes breaking trail. I lean back and cup my mouth with my hands for a three-part howl out over a large alder and winterberry hollow, which should make good night-hunting for cottontails and snowshoe hares. Almost before I finish, a lone coyote responds, once. The coyote must be nearby and facing toward me, because its howl is loud and very clear. Then silence takes over everything again. The thicket is a lowland tangle of branches bathed in blue moonlight that shines even more brightly in the distance off the flat, frozen surface of Loon Lake.

The coyote continues hunting, and I head for home.

Winter Storm

IT MIGHT SURPRISE SOMEONE who doesn't live in Canada to learn that the wake of an "Arctic cold front" in this country rarely means stormy winter weather. Instead, Arctic air masses most often bring smoky-pink sunrises, sunny clear days with long blue shadows, cold pale-yellow sunsets, and crisp starry nights—all featuring subzero temperatures. Fifty-six degrees below zero is the coldest I've personally experienced.

No, the real wind and snow almost always come when an Arctic front meets a low-pressure system laden with moisture from the continental southwest, and usually carried on an east wind. Without fail, a freshening breeze with wet gray-blue clouds on the eastern horizon at Loon Lake means "Get ready for something interesting."

This day in February started brewing before sunrise. One by one, the stars faded and winked out as a dark cloudbank—dark even against the night sky—rolled in from the east. The constellation Virgo disappeared around four a.m., and by dawn all that was left of Auriga (the Charioteer) was his white alpha star Capella, burning stubbornly in the northwest.

Sunrise was an undramatic event—more like a leaden lightening of uniform gray.

I decided to join the rest of the natural world by cramming what activity I could, in their case a quick search for food and in mine a short walk, before we all hunkered down for the inevitable. By late morning, I returned from my walk through heavy snowflakes that were gently descending vertically. By noon they were slanting westward. And by midafternoon, my cabin was engulfed in a howling winter whiteout.

I've experienced storms in all seasons—out on lakes and rivers, deep in the bush, inside a tent, even under the shelter of an overturned canoe tipped up against the wind. But there is something particularly satisfying about gazing out on winter's rage from the warmth and safety of a secure, warm cabin. The stove may back-puff in the gusts, the candle flame may flutter at night, but I know I'm basically well provided for and left with only a few simple things to do—sit tight, keep the fire burning, and wait the storm out.

This one blows unceasingly for the rest of the afternoon. Nothing ventures outside. Everything seeks shelter. The snow, though driven, also swirls into swelling drifts that seal my cabin into an envelope of natural insulation and jar the door. I look out my window, searching the scene before me for a glimpse of nearby Loon Lake that variously appears and disappears. The cabin roof, stringers, and rafters shudder in the wild snowsqualls and heavy gusts.

At night, I stoke a stove connected to a chimney that extends out into the cold blast itself, so I can imagine the glowing sparks being ripped horizontally downwind into the dark, along with the odd shingle. I have no choice; my very dreams include the wind.

By noon on the second day, I wonder whether this storm is even capable of fatigue. It roars its answer defiantly through the screened porch, driving more and more snow over the firewood I have stacked there. Just when I think I sense some weakening, a steady deep-throated power rolls across the land and brings the full force of Canadian winter to bear on my tiny shelter.

The wind totally obliterates the horizon, unifying land and sky. Now there is no telling whether the blended mass I see out my window is fallen snow lifted up into the air, or new snow driven down from above. For a moment, I feel genuinely threatened by the deafening wild violence all around me, and I wonder whether my cabin will be able to withstand its force.

But by midafternoon things finally begin to subside. Not suddenly. Not willingly. But with intermittent blasts that become less frequent, resolving into a streaming flow of windblown powder sweeping steadily and smoothly over everything in its path.

Then, finally, there's a hard-won silence. ...

My cabin door is blocked by snow on the outside, so I clamber out a window, step into a thigh-deep snowdrift, liberate a shovel by hand-digging under the floorboards, then dig out my entrance. I also clear a place on the front stoop, just to sit and take in the winter storm's aftermath, a cup of fresh steaming coffee in hand. ...

Before me is a world transformed, so beautifully clean and sculpted that I seriously weigh whether it is right to mar its surface with my tracks. In the end, I conclude that if the grouse and otter have ventured out from their shelters, as evidenced by their footprints, then so may I. The same winter's force that held me cabin-bound for two days has now given way to a soft gloaming, and reshaped a land waiting to be reanimated by all of us who live here.

Snowlife

I CAN'T REMEMBER exactly how I learned to read tracks
and bush sign. It seems to be something you either grow up
with or you don't. As a youngster, I remember carrying
lunch and a few loose shells in my father's rucksack as I
tagged along on moose hunts. He would show me the tracks
of huge hooves splayed deep in the half mud/half snow
along logging roads in early winter. And I so wanted the
droppings we also found to be fresh that I imagined every
pile was still steaming! Tempering the excitement of the hunt
was Dad's warning: "The fun stops when the moose goes
down"—a reference to the exhausting hard work involved
in field-dressing and packing one of these mammoths out of
a swamp far off any beaten path. Today, I can still call cows
and bulls in close during the rut. But I'm content to leave
them standing, and to watch "the south end of a moose
going north" when it realizes it has been fooled and crashes
back into the alders.

I do know that, however the skill of reading bush sign is
acquired, no book can teach it, or at least not very well. After
a while, these things register more or less unconsciously,
and your attention is drawn more to what's unusual or the
exception to the rule. You notice what isn't quite right. That
keeps the learning interesting and ongoing. Furthermore, I
believe your knowledge moves in stages, from simply
learning what made a certain track, to asking what the animal
was doing, and why.

Winter, obviously, is an excellent time for reading tracks, because, except during the iciest conditions, it's impossible for anything to move over the snow without leaving a trace of some kind. However, winter sign changes dramatically with freezing, thawing, melting, slumping, blowing, and, of course, falling snow.

Some of my favorites at Loon Lake are: braided lines of grouse tracks, especially a pair crisscrossing as they randomly roam the woods, take off, land, or explode from their snow burrows; a solitary otter, walking, bounding, then sliding over hilly country between frozen beaver ponds where it investigates every beaver lodge and food pile; cottontail rabbit night highways, dotted with droppings and beaten through lowland thickets too dense for humans to penetrate; the smudgy mark a coyote's hindquarters left as it sat down on a rocky ridge to take in the view the night before; the clean straight line left by a fox daintily placing its trailing paws exactly where the lead ones have stepped; the short trip of a red squirrel, barely a hand's-width out and back from the base of a tree it descended to dig up a cached cone; tail-drag between the neat prints of a white-footed mouse; the tiny twin footprints of a weasel rippling over the snow, hunting mice (a case of the predator's tracks being barely larger than the prey's); blood-stained urine in the heel-prints of a female porcupine plowing along during late winter, indicating she's ready to breed; the delicate wing-prints of a chickadee landing with hopping feet in search of any morsel to help it through the winter; snowshoe rabbit tracks distorted to the size of saucers by a January thaw; and snow fleas congregating in the warmth of my own boot prints.

This is a personal sampling of life on top of the snow. But consider the universe *beneath* winter's blanket. No one has written more knowledgeably about this sub-nivean world than Canadian zoologist W.O. Pruitt Jr., who describes a fascinating micro-environment where "there is no cycle of light and darkness, no rise and fall of temperature, no moon, no warble of pine grosbeak or hoot of owl. ..."

Here is where small mammals such as voles carry on their busy winter lives, scuttling through murky leaf-matted tunnels and runways that become apparent to us surface-dwellers only when the snow decays. This is the complex world of life-giving gas-and-heat exchanges, tinkling crystals, and lattice-lined pathways to stored food. Here mini-hothouses incubate insects and other invertebrate populations that kick-start the food chain in spring. It stands to reason that all resident life forms in the Northern Hemisphere have adapted to different qualities of snow, but to hear Pruitt tell it, we humans have been downright deprived by being condemned to the surface!

Many beautiful snow traces are not from animals at all, but from dried leaves blown lightly cartwheeling over the top, low-hanging branches that score patterns on the surface, temperature craters melted in the lee of tree-trunk bases, heavier snow falling in clumps from boughs above, brittle branches and bits of bark broken off by high winds, and thousands of pitted indents caused by rain or a warm spell.

Energetic arboreal feeders, especially squirrels, are perpetually showering the winter forest floor with seed husks, cone scales, or tender twigs with buds from above; porcupines gnaw entire branches and tree tops from gray to white by eating the bark; and woodpeckers send down shards of dead wood as they root about for goodies such as overwintering bugs and larvae.

Snow, far from being a monotonous blank area of white, is in fact a living ledger in which winter posts its journal entries, occasionally wiping the page clean, then busily beginning another account. It serves as an insulative layer, without which hundreds of species could never survive winter, and as a vital frozen reservoir of moisture made available by the warming temperatures of spring. Each six-sided snowflake on my parka is unduplicated and wonderful in itself. But when they combine to form a winter blanket over the land, a miracle emerges.

Winter Birds

OF THE 115 BIRD SPECIES I've recorded so far at Loon Lake, twenty-four, or roughly one-fifth, are resident all winter. There's something hardily Canadian about this bunch who stay behind to tough it out with the rest of us. They constitute an elite—the one bird in five that has adapted to temperature extremes that would overwhelm the other eighty percent, who need to maintain acceptable living conditions by moving south.

My favorites are the chickadees and nuthatches, which seem to be always energetic and travel nomadically together, along with both hairy and downy woodpeckers. When absolutely nothing else is willing to venture forth in winter, chances are you'll glimpse some or all of these.

In *A Sand County Almanac*, Aldo Leopold distilled the chickadee into "a small bundle of large enthusiasms." W. Earl Godfrey in *Birds of Canada* rhetorically asks, "Who ever saw a dejected chickadee?" This is the tiny dynamo most likely to be first attracted to a bird feeder, yet compared with, say, finches, which linger to feed, chickadees usually grab a morsel and whimsically disappear somewhere else to actually eat it. Then they flit back for another. It's as if chickadees were duty-bound to put four times as much sheer effort as anyone else into the most routine activity. Chickadees are rarely encountered, because they always seem to do the encountering, roaming in loose wandering troupes that discover the human traveler as we tramp through the bush or pause for a rest. Then they vanish as mysteriously as they appeared. "Chick-a-dee-dee-dee" is a frisky, familiar, and uplifting birdcall at any time of the year, but the drawn-out spring call, "fee-bee" (just a few notes short of the white-throated sparrow's summer song), is particularly welcome in late winter. This "fluffy, confiding little bird," says Godfrey, is "the personification of cheerfulness and good nature," which no doubt accounts for Leopold's dry observation that "... weather is the only killer so devoid of both humor and dimension as to kill a chickadee."

And why did the North see fit to produce two sets of winter birds, one of nuthatches and another of woodpeckers, that so closely resemble each other?

The larger white-breasted nuthatch is a sleek, dapper, short-tailed bird, with clean blocks of color, including a slate-blue back reminiscent of rain-filled clouds. If the mouse-like brown creeper can only skulk *up* a tree, the upside-down nuthatch knows no such limitation as it descends, spirals, hangs, and traverses tightly against trunks and limbs. Although no written rendering can do justice to any bird's call, I find every author's version of this nuthatch's voice to be totally beyond my experience. There are references in the literature to notes and whistles described variously as "yank, hit, tew, whi, who and tootoo," but not one to the nasal "nerm, nerm, nerm" which I always hear, uttered almost under its breath and usually in the company of chickadees. To a nuthatch, this simply seems to mean that its world is unfolding as it should.

The delicate red-breasted nuthatch, at two-thirds the size, has a breeding and winter range at least three times as large and much further north in Canada than its larger cousin, proving that size alone doesn't always give you a jump on survival. This is a more boreal bird, which has bequeathed us two mysteries: (1) What purpose is served by the pitch smeared around the entrance to its nest hole? (2) How best to describe that subtle burnished color on its underparts? The prize goes to Godfrey for "ochraceous buff."

Hairy woodpeckers are simply larger versions of downies, with a proportionately longer bill. Males of both species have a smart red bar on the nape that is equally capable of catching a bright morning's sun or dull afternoon's light in winter. Hairies are likely to announce your unexpected arrival with a loud "squeak," followed by undulating flight to some slightly more distant point. On the other hand, if they're busy at work and either unaware of or unconcerned about your presence, they stay close to provide a muffled pecking and movement among dead trees that may well be the only signs of life to keep you company in midwinter.

Downies are not only one-third smaller than hairies, but also quieter, subtler, and equally at home in new forest or old field. For example, downy woodpeckers have been known to feast on goldenrod gall fly larvae which develop in round, marble-sized growths along the stems of these old field plants. A neat hole in the middle of a gall means the developed adult gall fly managed to work its way out to freedom from within, whereas a shattered one means the overwintering larva was evacuated by the beak and searching tongue of a downy.

Black-capped chickadees, white-breasted and red-breasted nuthatches, hairy and downy woodpeckers—the five "tree-circlers"—are joined by a select group of other winter birds who provide color, life, and companionship under the most demanding conditions. Thank you, all.

Orion's Sky

ALTHOUGH SCIENCE tells us it is not strictly correct, just as a harvest moon appears to be gloriously large, the entire canopy of stars in winter appears to be crisply brighter than in any other season. It's always difficult to accept as truth an explanation that defies human experience, and even more difficult to judge when we should do so. Optical illusions aside, winter does put on display some of the most luminous star members of our Milky Way galaxy, measured

objectively by astronomers using the "magnitude scale."
So, to this extent, what the eye beholds is at least partially
confirmed by science.

Above all, I believe that an interest in astronomy and
becoming a "naturalist of the night" profoundly expands
one's point of view. For instance, by tracking the planets
we can follow what's happening in our home solar system,
by studying stars and nebulas we can roam our home galaxy,
and by observing other galaxies we can step out beyond our
immediate home, in either sense, into deep space. All three
perspectives are available via the naked eye, when conditions
are right and if you know where to look. Further, if you are
inherently restless and yearn for a preview of the next
season, just stay up past midnight to view the sky as it will
appear in the early evening a few months hence—a
wonderful winter remedy for "cabin fever."

My own interest in astronomy began when I was a young
boy delivering the now-defunct *Winnipeg Tribune*. Since I
lived in a remote hydro camp in northwestern Ontario, the
paper had to be shipped in by rail, so it arrived a day late.
Therefore I delivered newspapers to my trailer-camp route
very early in the morning the day after they were actually
published. Picking them up involved a long walk through
the bush, which left me alone with the night sky, especially
in winter.

One Christmas morning I felt particularly hard done by,
because, while everyone else was waking up to presents under
the tree, I had to go to work. It was crisp and very cold, so,
to make matters worse, I could feel frostbite relentlessly
settling into my toes and fingers. Then, I glanced up.

To me, the northern lights had never been so spectacular. They weren't just flooding up from one horizon, as usual, but seemed to be bursting out radially in lime-green waves from a central point in the dark canopy above me. Long bands of neon color shot across the sky, then shifted and blended into one another as a backdrop for the next influx of bright boreal fire.

I dropped my paper carrier's bag and stood still, literally gaping up at such a heavenly panorama. I felt head-to-toe awestruck and, like the biblical shepherds, "sore afraid." In fact, looking to the east, I was fully expecting a blinding star and chorus of angels to appear at any moment!

I hurried to finish my paper route, and rushed home excitedly to tell my family what I had seen. But it was daylight now, the Second Coming was apparently over, and everyone was more interested in the day's festivities. In hindsight, I regard the whole experience as a secret shared only between the stars and me. It was a performance orchestrated just for me, a special gift for a cold young boy who was feeling sorry for himself, but who in fact was lucky not to have been indoors with everyone else on that dark and early Christmas morning.

The riches of the night sky are freely and democratically available to everyone. All that is needed is a penchant to observe, a dark sky (not easily found these days), and a functioning pair of night-adapted eyes, which unaided, as God gave them to us, are capable of seeing some 3,000 distinct stars. A good teacher certainly helps, either in person or by way of a useful book. Terence Dickinson, for example, has been deservedly awarded the Order of Canada for drawing thousands of people to the stars through his popular writing, especially his regularly revised book, *Nightwatch*. A decent pair of 7 by 50 or 10 by 50 binoculars, affordable to most people, will significantly enhance your night watching experience (and, incidentally, put you on a technical par with Galileo). Binoculars make thousands more stars available to the human eye, and also provide the best wide-angle views of such heavenly objects as the rich field of individual stars that otherwise appear as dust in the Milky Way; double stars that appear as singles; and star clusters, nebulas, and extraordinary comets such as Hyutake and Hale-Bopp, with their gas and dust tails extending out many degrees across the sky. Finally, if your interest and pocketbook are sufficient, a good telescope with motor-drive—to automatically track star movement as night progresses—will transport you literally out of this world into a time zone that ignores any earthbound clock.

Overlooking Loon Lake is a rocky knoll that lifts me a few meters closer to the night sky, and serves as my wide-open observatory. It is fully equipped with a wooden chair, small red flashlight, star atlas, binoculars, and my eight-inch (200-mm) Schmidt-Cassegrain telescope lovingly disassembled and dragged in on my toboggan during winter. Many's the owl, I'm sure, that has peered inquiringly out from the forest into this opening at a solitary hunched figure, quietly shuffling sky charts for night journeys out and beyond.

As for the winter stars themselves, there can be little doubt that the most readily identified starting point is Orion (the Hunter), with his three-star belt (Alnitak, Alnilam, and

Mintaka) and dangling sword. The entire constellation is outlined by Orion's "four corner" stars: Betelgeuse, Bellatrix, Rigel, and Saiph. Once this basic constellation is located, the entire southern part of the winter sky can be determined by various sight lines, using Orion's constituent stars, including the constellations of Lepus (the Rabbit under Orion's feet), Canis Major and Canis Minor (the loyal Dog Stars always following the Hunter), Gemini (the Twins), Auriga (the Charioteer), Taurus (the Bull), and Perseus (the Hero). Within this assemblage of constellations are five bright marker stars known as the Winter Arc: gleaming blue Capella in Auriga directly overhead, arcing to Castor and Pollux in Gemini, down to Procyon in Canis Minor, then to brilliant Sirius—the brightest winter star, at magnitude minus 4, burning white in Canis Major. On a slightly overcast winter night, when the detail and dimmer stars of the constellations are lost, often the Winter Arc persists and can still be seen.

The middle "star" in Orion's sword is in fact not a star at all, but the Orion Nebula—a magnificent gaseous star nursery 20,000 times the diameter of our entire solar system, with what Dickinson describes as "four blue jewels embedded in a delicate celestial cloud" at its center. This is called the Trapezium, visible best by telescope. I've spent entire evenings never straying from Orion because of its rich field of double stars and swirling nebulas. Orion also stalks the morning sky before dawn in autumn, which gives him special meaning to more earthbound hunters headed out to duck blinds or deer stands before sunrise. His spirit literally presides over the fall hunt.

If Orion anchors the southern winter sky, then Ursa Major (the Great Bear or the Big Dipper) serves the same purpose for the northern sector. Using sight lines from stars in this constellation, we can readily identify Queen Cassiopeia and her royal husband, Cepheus; Ursa Minor (the Little Bear), which includes Polaris (the North Star); Draco (the Dragon), whose immense curving tail wriggles up between the Big and Little Dippers; Leo (the Lion), and Cancer, which contains Praesepe, also called the "Beehive"—my favorite star cluster.

One unforgettable night (my log indicates it was December 29, 1994), I was out early enough (7:45 p.m.) to behold what is usually an autumnal constellation, Cygnus (the Swan), also known as the Northern Cross, "... with its alpha-star Daneb shining at the top of the crucifix, standing upright in the Milky Way as a background curtain to the northwest, absolutely beautiful and strong, majestic, and breathtaking, rooted at the far end of Loon Lake." Such are the rewards of winter stargazing.

The winter west in evening is a particularly beckoning region, because therein lie the constellations Pegasus and the Triangulum, which direct the eye to our closest galaxies— Andromeda and M33 (the Triangulum Galaxy)—both visible to the naked eye on a deep, dark night. The light we see from Andromeda began its journey some 2.5 million years ago. These two weak smudges are in fact companion galaxies to our own Milky Way, spirals made up of hundreds of billions of stars and no doubt even more planets, light years beyond every other star we can see with the unaided eye.

It is fascinating to realize that our seasonal night skies today are virtually no different from those experienced by all of humankind. Only our cosmologies have changed. For example, ancient thinkers held that the stars were in fact glimpses of infinite fire perceived through tiny holes in a protective, revolving dome encasing our world. This thought came to mind when I traveled home overnight by rail in CP's famous Dome Car. I sat up high and alone all night, gazing at stars piercing through my own crystalline, windowed ceiling, and waved to night watchmen whisking by on the wooden platforms of dimly lit old train stations shrouded in ice fog. The stars and stations were left swirling in dry clouds of snow swept up by a speeding train.

These same stars have guided people and animals alike in their travels over land and sea for centuries. But the ordinary citizens of past civilizations were much more sensitively attuned than we are to any changes against this stellar backdrop, for example, the arrival, phases, and ecliptic paths of the moon and planets. The Universe is still out there, persisting and available to all of us, the birthplace of our own nuclear furnace—the Sun, our planet, and therefore ourselves. How ironic that something so wonderful and fundamentally formative goes largely unappreciated and unseen, washed out by artificial light from the cities where most of modern humanity now dwells.

Walking on Water

READING ICE IS LIKE EATING wild mushrooms: Just when you think you know what you're doing, you make a mistake—which could be fatal. When in doubt, I've always preferred to let others pick mushrooms, and I walk on ice only when absolutely confident it's safe (even then, I carry a sturdy pole to lever myself out should I break through). C.H.D. Clarke, one of the ablest and most experienced outdoorsmen in Ontario, drowned after falling through the ice.

Still, walking on the frozen ponds and lakes around Loon Lake is irresistible, because it provides both ease of travel and an entirely different perspective on the rest of the landscape—a vantage point not possible during other seasons. Yes, I paddle the lakes in summer. But there's something about being out there, standing on water and looking back onto the land, that turns everything around.

On the ponds, I can saunter like a coyote right past the tops of beaver food piles frozen offshore into the ice, and snoop around their lodges from the same side that the beaver normally enter underwater. I can imagine a spring drake wood duck, out there under a drowned buttonbush, putting on a fine display for a pretty hen. Or I can cut my travel time in half by taking a shortcut over flat, firm routes that in spring-summer-fall are impassable to anything but the likes of a beaver, a wood duck, or a good Labrador retriever.

I remember one crisp cold day in February, when Sherry and I went skating on Loon Lake. Its surface was randomly blotched by glare ice and blown snow. The challenge, and pleasure, was to find a continuous path on the former without encountering the latter, something like happy rats negotiating a glassy maze. I know I cheated once or twice when I avoided a dead end by leaping over a patch of snow to land once again on bare ice. But in the end we managed to puzzle our way across the entire width of the lake on shiny hard surfaces. With our lungs full of fresh, cold air, and the trees literally popping like the crack of a rifle in the subzero temperatures, it was exhilarating to feel winter within and around us!

One practical reason for being out on Loon Lake in winter is to fetch water. This I do manually, using a long, heavy ice pick, something all those who think water simply comes out of a tap should wield at least once in their lives. First, I choose a spot safely far enough out from shore to avoid any organic material that could be stirred up from the lake bottom. Next, and most important, the hole must be started large enough to allow for tapering as I chip down through the ice. The later in winter, and the thicker the ice, the larger the starting circle has to be. My rule of thumb is to start the hole about twice as wide as I judge the ice to be thick. A good pick, especially one with a weighted working end, makes the job a lot easier.

After brushing away surface snow with my mitts, I begin to chop into the top ice, which is always white and air-filled, stopping only long enough to clean out chips and chunks as I go. The middle ice is light blue and denser. But I know I'm really getting somewhere when I hit the super-compressed ice that appears dark blue–black in the hole, and skitters hard and clear when I toss chunks of it out onto the surface. There's a rewarding moment at the end when my pick first punches into the lake, and water rushes up to fill the hole. A loose grip or slippery wet mitts at this point could, and have, cost me my ice pick.

Sometimes the lake for some distance around the hole "talks back" as under-ice pressures are released through the hole. I like to chip the base of the hole to about six inches (15 cm) wide, then I rake the slush and ice chunks off the water's surface with an ice skimmer, and fill my pails with a dipper. Washing my face in this ice water right away, back in the cabin, is an act of sheer courage.

On a cold winter night the lake reclaims my water hole within an hour, with a film of ice that steadily thickens until my pick is needed to reopen it in the morning. I take this as a courteous reminder from the lake itself as to how it should be at this time of the year, which is to say how it was before I arrived, and how it will be again after I leave.

Steaming Horses

ONE BRIGHT WINTER MORNING, Archie Walker delivered a face cord of firewood to the cabin by horse-drawn sleigh. This team and sleigh were the same ones Archie used to log the elm swamp, so the whole outfit included a sturdy, open, hardwood box, built especially to haul wood. The image of those two heavy workhorses, warm and steaming in the dead of winter only a few paces from the cabin door, has never left me.

Francis, Archie's son, tells me now that both horses were females—Polly, a gray mare, and Doll, a younger black filly who never did have a foal. I remember the huge leather collar around the strong neck of each horse, the yoke across in front of them, the long wooden tongue down between them back to the sleigh, and the whiffletree across behind. I remember an intricate system of lines, traces, guides, buckles, clips, snaps, and swivels, which was incomprehensible to me but second nature to both Archie and his horses. I remember the small farm dog, Max, who gaily followed the sleigh in, then guarded it loyally, lying underneath when it was stopped and growling at anyone who approached too close. But most of all, I remember the *sound* of that team and sleigh—the jangle of the harness, the heavy thud of wide hooves, the slide of the runners, and the soft commands from Archie as the whole unit went to work through the snow.

I suppose that seeing heavy workhorses hitched up today brings with it an overwhelmingly nostalgic sense of history. Were Polly and Doll's ancestors among the first horses the Algonquins ever saw, accompanying Europeans to this land? Did these same bloodlines skid wood out to landings during the days of the lumber barons, including the Rathbun Lumber Company of Deseronto, which once owned this very property? Did they help provide sufficient "improvements," by pulling out stumps and plowing small pockets of soil, for settlers and homesteaders to take permanent title to their lots? Did they haul cedar posts and split rails for fences; quarried limestone for churches; hardwood ties for the railway; huge timbers for dams; heavy grinding wheels for mills; and wagonload after wagonload of lumber for stores, barns, and homes? How much of this hard work, I wonder, was genetically encoded in the bone, muscle, and blood of the two horses that stood so gently at my cabin doorstep?

After we tossed and kicked the last of the firewood out of the sleigh box, Archie put Polly and Doll into reverse, then headed out with Max in happy pursuit. Their hindquarters, bobbing easily ahead of a light empty sleigh up and over the top of our treed hill, were the last I ever saw of that team. They were sold after Archie died, says Francis, and he thinks the harness is hanging in a shed somewhere in the next township.

Rest

WINTER IS A SEASON of rest. Most resident plants, trees, insects, reptiles, amphibians, fish, birds, and mammals at Loon Lake have adapted to that fact. Some go dormant or hibernate, some remain active, others leave for destinations farther south. Similarly, while some humans do their best to avoid winter, others embrace it. Gilles Vigneault's moving song declares, "Mon pays, c'est n'est pas un pays, c'est l'hiver" ("My country, it's not a county, it's winter").

Nationalism aside, winter offers each of us a rare taste of true silence—the chance to be alone with nothing but our own heartbeat. I hear it when I pause from snowshoeing in the bush; I hear it when I cross frozen lakes and ponds; I hear it when I step outside my cabin at midnight; and I hear it between the howls of a coyote and the crackles of a warming fire.

The opportunity for silence and solitude is steadily being eroded from human experience in all but the most remote regions of our planet. Winter in the North offers a brave last refuge.

Spring

MARCH – MAY

Sleeping Giants

Half Loads and High Water

April Geese against the Moon

Forest Flowers

On Your Own Power

Earth Day, April 22

Snoozing Porcupines and Soughing Pines

On Patience

Morning Coffee on the Front Stoop

Renewal

Sleeping Giants

FOR ANYONE ATTUNED to the land, the question of when one season ends and another begins is somewhat meaningless. One simply blends into the other. Such a state of flux, or perpetual transition, leaves you reasonably certain of what season you're in, but not when it started or will end. All of this is particularly true of spring.

For example, does spring begin in late January, when the first migrating horned larks are heard like tiny bells high over snow-covered cultivated fields? Not likely, because there are still two months of rock-frozen ground and blowing snow ahead.

Does spring begin in February, when the great horned owls nest in the crown of a big white pine? Perhaps not, because those hardy owlets will live in that snowy loft for a good month yet, under a tent formed by the adults' wings, snuggling in close for body heat on clear, below-zero nights.

Is spring here when tracks in the snow signal that the first chipmunks have emerged early from their winter torpor to mate? Or with the sight of a carefree pair of foxes playing in a forest opening? Or with the pungent meanderings of an early wayward skunk? Probably not, because all of these are likely to re-enter their dens for a while yet, while young chipmunks, foxes, and skunks gestate within.

Is it spring when crows become noticeably more active, and gulls forage on winter-kill further inland? Maybe. But both crows and gulls have been busy doing this on nice days earlier in the year, and will continue to do so for months afterwards.

How about when the first male redwing blackbird is heard over dry bulrushes, staking out his territory before the flush of females arrives from the south? Well, yes, but chances are that by now the grackles, killdeer, and robins are also with him, or not far behind. In which case we're no longer debating the beginning of spring, because it is already well under way.

I have concluded that the beginning of spring is entirely a matter of personal opinion. So here is mine: spring arrives on the wind during the first sunny afternoon in March.

At Loon Lake, I've most often felt this breeze through woodsmoke, while brewing tea over a fire on a south-facing slope. Not far away are the first brown patches of sun-dried leaves, surrounded by granular spring "corn snow," which spells the end of powdery drifts for another year. Chances are it's warm enough to tend the fire in shirtsleeves, and my homemade lamp-wick snowshoe harness hangs loose and wet, not freeze-formed as it would have been a week earlier. There is sun on my face, and spring on the wind.

"Who has seen the wind?" asks W.O. Mitchell. "Neither you nor I" is his answer. But we have all *felt* it. I think spring, too, is felt. Not seen or announced clearly by anything in particular, but wafted in subtly on that first sunny afternoon in March.

In fact, the soft vernal wind is the front end of a large, warm tide of life sweeping the American continents from south to north. One huge sleeping giant in the North is taking a slow, deep inward breath, drawing an abundance of living things up from the South—everything from butterflies to birds to whales—all moving north to breed, reproduce, and grow during summer. This northern giant's work is complemented perfectly by a southern giant who at the same time slowly breathes out, exhaling the tide of life northward, hastening it on its way, having harbored and nourished it over winter. In fall, of course, roles are reversed —the hemispheric giants on different sides of the equator exchange breaths again, this time exhaling life from the North and inhaling southward. Thus, ancient lungs breathe one complete breath a year, working to ensure that thousands of wildlife species, by moving, continually occupy suitable habitat. My cabin on Loon Lake experiences this vital slipstream something like a piece of ocean kelp: entirely subject to more fundamental currents, but master of none. Spring is but one phase of this flowing global tide, borne on a shared breath in March.

Conservation biologists confirm that spring is created by a miracle every bit as wonderful as the synchronized breathing of sleeping giants. I'm referring to "photoperiod," or length of daylight. Photoperiod has been scientifically shown to be the underlying cue for many changes in the natural world, especially migration. Factors such as warming temperatures and thawing lakes may temper the tide of life, but it is set in motion and ultimately driven by photoperiod interacting with hormones and other biochemicals found in plants and animals alike.

Changing length of day is brought about in turn by the fact that our Earth is tipped on its axis, accounting for longer and shorter days in the Northern and Southern hemispheres as the planet carves its annual orbit around the Sun. Therefore, what we experience as simple observations of the spring season—buds becoming leaves and geese flooding north—are in fact wonderful adaptations to an astronomical accident.

It may help to remember, the next time you despair of spring ever arriving, that it *must* come—its inevitability is written in the stars themselves.

Half Loads and High Water

IN MARCH, the "half load" signs go up on unpaved backcountry roads, and in April high water inevitably follows.

The half-load signs are an example of government advising us of the obvious: that frost is coming out of the ground, therefore this road is soft, therefore heavy trucks are legally restricted to half their normal load. This is when your tires squish, wallow, and wander, to take a vehicle pretty much wherever spring fancies rather than where the driver wants. It's also when the leaf springs and bench seats of an old pickup give new meaning to words like "frost heave, pothole, rut," and "an honest ride." Pulling over to let an oncoming vehicle pass boils down to judging just how soft that road shoulder really is, and exactly where it slumps or drops off beyond the point of no return.

Still, the posting of half-load signs subtly signals something more elemental—a change of season, and the date by which certain chores should be under way, maybe mundane spring cleaning, or maybe taking a good flyline off the reel to let it straighten and relax in anticipation of trout season opening in a month's time.

High water is the autograph of spring. To be sure, the signature varies according to snow load, rainfall, and the timing of warming temperatures. But there *will* be high water to one degree or another. And thank God there is, because this ecological flush of moisture often determines what will live or die for the rest of the year.

High water, of course, is not unrelated to half loads. For example, this is the time when the beaver rush to rebuild dams in order to stem the spring tide. Their construction jobs often flood roads, a situation that is resolved by the municipal road maintenance crew using shovels and, if necessary, dynamite. The beaver return to take advantage of a strategically placed culvert to dam and hold the flow, flooding the road again. The road crew retaliates by ripping the beavers' handiwork apart and replacing it with an old steel bed frame spread across the culvert to keep the beaver out. The beaver return to weave their fresh cuttings through the wires and helical springs of the bed frame, then apply finishing touches of packed mud to flood the road all over again. Back and forth, move and counter-move, like two old-timers playing cribbage on the porch, the time-honored rivalry is played out more by tradition than with any real hostility. I believe the beaver more often than not gain the upper hand, as any aerial photo will testify. Still, it's ironic: this industrious creature was honored as our national emblem because it helped "build the country" by literally sacrificing the skin off its back; exploited almost to extinction, it became the subject of re-introductions, which were so successful that it is now regarded as little more than a local nuisance.

High water signals that it is time to look for pike spawning upstream in creeks that have backed up into shallow flooded fields. It is also the time when Archie Walker used to net and pickle white suckers while their flesh was still firm and capable of sustaining his family. High water provides life-giving melt pools for insect larvae and hatched adults that serve as food for spring peepers and other amphibians that depend on early invertebrates for survival. Those same first generations of insects tide over migrating drab flycatchers and colorful wood warblers alike. High water is needed to flood the roots of everything from cottonwood trees and red maples to the nascent wild cardinal flower (preparing the ground for resplendent crimson blooms in August). High water softens the soil for the earthworms that are probed by the long supple beaks of migrating woodcocks, who entertain me on April evenings from my cabin screened porch with their mating calls and sky dance. High water provides enough clearance over boulders to paddle whitewater on rivers in spring that will be reduced to rubble and little more than sluggish cow creeks in summer. And high water ensures a puddle, no matter how humble, in every corner of the county, for a handsome drake mallard and his hen.

Half loads and high water are both happenings and harbingers. They stand as events in their own right, and they bespeak events yet to come. They are glanced at in a rearview mirror, and they are felt in our bones.

April Geese against the Moon

EVERY ONCE IN A WHILE an image like a nostalgic Terry Redlin waterfowl painting freeze-frames itself in real life, so perfect and moving that life becomes art in those moments, and we experience what Quetico guide and author Sigurd F. Olson called "the singing wilderness." Such is the image of April geese against the moon.

There's something elemental about what Leopold called the "wild poem" of migrating geese. They float along bearing the soul of spring and fall. I've watched thousands of geese rise in a deafening cloud from the muddy expanse of the Fraser River delta in British Columbia. I've seen my grandfather, busy working in the fields of Saskatchewan, stop and shut down his tractor just to look up and listen. I once skipped a morning session of the annual meeting of the Manitoba Naturalists' Society to watch spring snow geese pour into the frozen, straw-colored Oak Hammock Marsh north of Winnipeg. And I know that the coastal Cree, who live along Hudson Bay, experience that same stirring when the very first flock of Canadas arrives in late March. They taught me how to call and decoy snows and blues in September, along tidal flats unequalled in the world for their biological richness—something you can taste in the geese themselves. I've flown over James Bay for days in twin-engine Otters, looking down on suspended undulating ribbons of geese wafting south—an unforgettable perspective on the birds against the habitat that gave them life. I've witnessed half a dozen "suits" with briefcases in downtown

Toronto shade their eyes with their free hand for a wistful glimpse of wildness. I've experienced the spectacle of bright Arctic snow geese pitching into Cap-Tourmente on the North Shore of the St. Lawrence River in Quebec, flashing white against the russet-red backdrop of eastern hardwoods in full autumn color. Here the hunters in fall still move out to pit blinds at low tide, using traditional horse-drawn mud sleighs. All of which is testimony to something profoundly magnetic and evocative about this particular current in the tide of life moving seasonally up and down our hemisphere. It reaches deep inside us to conjure up images of where the geese have been and where they are going. Perhaps we long to be there with them.

On this night in April, I am quietly cooking dinner on my woodstove. I hear them, faint at first. But after a long day that began somewhere south of the border, they are bearing down with determination and wings set for an ice-free bay, now gleaming in full moonlight on Loon Lake. The resting place is finally in sight, and they will be here in seconds. Walter and Splash, my two Labrador retrievers, lift their heads from a deep sleep on their warm rug by the stove. Together, we all step outside onto fresh frozen ground.

Flaring, dipping, and descending, the geese sail directly over my cabin to stage for the night. Perhaps a hundred birds glide by the moon and a curtain of spring stars. First I hear raucous honking, then quiet as wings are set for the last time on this day, then the wind roaring resistance through braking pinions. Next comes the long splashdown of spreading feet, the keel of their breasts and the rest of their tired bodies. Then, more honking to help guide and reassure the remainder of the flock on their way in. When all have landed safely, someone is elected scout to watch for danger during the night, and with no further fanfare ... silence.

No one arriving seconds after them could have known that the hearts of a hundred wild geese were resting on Loon Lake that night. But of course that's exactly how they wanted it, for tomorrow meant another lap on the way north ... and home.

Forest Flowers

IT ALL BEGINS against the snows of late February when willows start to turn yellow-ocher, the fine branches on birches show a tinge of dark red, and dogwoods deepen to a rich burgundy. Soon after, the first skunk cabbages poke up purple and green through black earth in low spots, and the freeze-thaw of night-day sets maple sap in motion. Now, when the land is wet and mottled half brown/half white, it is ready to explode with new life.

Leopold claimed he could tell you a good deal about a person's "vocation, hobbies and general level of ecological education by the plant-birthdays he notices." At Loon Lake, the lesson is about to begin. In fact, the experienced eye could easily tell what month of the year it is upon seeing simply a square meter of the forest floor.

Hepaticas tell me it is early April, with pastel pink, lavender, and white blooms against rich, round-lobed leaves that remained green under the snow all winter, anticipating the first dry sunny afternoons of spring. These brave souls may last only a short time, but what a glorious entrance they usher in for spring. After the hepaticas flower, tiny purple-pink gaywings or fringed polygala appear, showing a complicated airplanelike bloom which has a miniature tube for a fuselage and two little wings springing up from both sides. These will persist on rich sites well into May and June. About the same time, yellow carpets of barren strawberry leaven bright new life into thickets and uplands. The small five-petalled flower is backed by sturdy, geranium-like leaves that, like the hardy hepatica, have survived winter. These three—hepaticas, gaywings, and barren strawberry—account for most of the early spring wildflower color at Loon Lake.

But now, look more closely. There, too, are the familiar white flower and yellow stamens of wild strawberry. Here and there are fragile white starflowers with golden anthers held aloft by delicate thin stems. This plant creates the illusion of a central white star framed by a green starburst of leaves when you look down on it from straight overhead.

Watch for subtle green flowers: exquisite blue bead lily reaching up yellow-green from the mud by the lake; spiked green hemispheres on wild sarsaparilla, about the size of melon balls beneath an umbrella of leaves that will turn the color of ripe cantaloupe in October; and the rodlike green spear, or "spadex," on arrow arum that embellishes beaver ponds.

Next trilliums, the defining woodland flowers of May, clutter upland sites everywhere under the fresh lime-green

mist of this year's tree buds. The large-flowered trillium
(*Trillium grandiflorum*) is most common, pure white at its
peak, and fading to pinkish and dull purple as the flower
wilts. "Never pick a trillium" is the admonition given to every
Ontario school child, not just because it is the provincial
flower, but because the rootstocks will often die if the leaves
or flower are removed. Painted trilliums (*Trillium undulatum*)
have narrower petals with dark pink brushed into their center
and veins. Trilliums are members of the lily family, bringing
their own grace to our forests after Easter.

Mid- to late-May features the most species of spring
wildflowers. The early ones linger; some are in full flush;
others build a bridge to summer. Minuscule green recurved
sepals and red stamens make up the delicate flower of Indian
cucumber root. Wild columbine nourishes nectar-seeking
spring insects and returning hummingbirds from its nodding
red and yellow bells held up for feasting by long stems. The
next time you admire the flower, also take time to notice
wild columbine leaves. They show a subtle cloudy hue as
if Nature stirred milk into her usual palette of fresh spring
green.

Clusters of tiny white bells, some of them inviting a
hand lens for close inspection, adorn everything from
wintergreen to blueberry bushes. Colonies of mayflower
carpet the uplands with zigzag stems, presenting clusters
of white star-shaped blooms, particularly beautiful when
strewn around the base of an old-growth pine. More solitary
white-petalled flowers are crafted by bunchberry, wood
anemones, bloodroot, and goldthread, whose yellow
underground roots were chewed by Indians and settlers to

cure cankers. A single white apple blossom-like flower appears on mayapple, between a pair of distinctive leaves resembling a big blotchy lake with long bays drawn on a topographic map. In swamps, water arum puts forth a single white leaflike spathe as backdrop for a phallic cluster of yellow flowers so microscopic they could be dust. Woolly pussy toes live up to their name, scattering white paws along dry open ridges, next to the small white funnel flowers clustered on bastard toadflax, which lives off nutrients from nearby trees and shrubs. Even the dreaded poison ivy manages loose random bunches of yellowish-white blooms along its stems.

These, along with many others, are the wildflowers celebrating spring at Loon Lake. Their thriving and waning are all tempered by the unique nature of each spring—early or late, wet or dry, warm or cold. But there is one magnificent plant that for me more than any other marks the passage of spring to summer: the pink lady's-slipper orchid.

At Loon Lake, this coveted wildflower (also known as the pink moccasin flower) occurs only in a couple of warm, well-drained locations. Every year, all year, I watch these plants go through their various life stages, from sprouting and blooming in May and June, to wilting in summer, to forming brownish seed pods that dry out and persist through fall and winter. The seeds are like dust. Pink lady's slippers are very difficult to propagate or grow in any form of domestic garden, so they are truly *wild* flowers to be left and entrusted unconditionally to the whims of Nature.

No technical or botanical description does justice to the beauty of the pink lady's slipper. The slender strong stalk bears one flower, rising from two verdant long oval leaves. To my eye, the flower itself more resembles the engorged pink sac of a breeding male (of any species) than a more discreet "lady's slipper," complete with venation and deep, crease-forming flaps, which divide the sac roughly in two. The sac's function is to trap pollinators, such as bees, which are drawn through the flaps literally to the "light at the end of the tunnel" near the flower's top, where pollen rubs off on their backs. This long main petal-pouch is capped by brown side-petals spreading out from the point where the stalk suspends the slipper. It is one of Canada's largest native orchids, and it is breathtaking. The bloom lasts only a couple of weeks, then shrivels to become quite unremarkable. To me, therefore, the pink lady's slipper epitomizes the hot blood of spring, a vernal climax that quickly subsides, diminishes, and surrenders to the droning hum of summer.

While wildflowers, like birds, have become the more obvious touchstone and passion of naturalists tapping into seasonal change, there is a less-noticed but equally splendid and colorful transformation taking place each spring at eye level in shrubs, and high above in the forest canopy. For trees and shrubs also "bloom" to reproduce, through all manner of catkins, pollen cones, and more commonly recognized "blossoms" or flowers.

At Loon Lake, red maple kick-starts this arboreal colorfest in mid-April. First the red buds lengthen and swell. Then yellow pollen flowers and red seed flowers emerge, usually on different branches of the same tree, often while snow still lingers on the hills. Soon a reddish haze engulfs the lowlands, even before leaves appear. Close inspection will reveal billions of red flowers—each with five tiny petals and sepals in bouquetlike groupings or clusters on stalks. All of this bud burst is impeccably cued to temperature and length of day.

Other, better-known tree and shrub flowers include the white blossoms of the introduced domestic apple and virtually all other fruit trees, as well as wild cherry, hawthorn, dogwood, viburnum, elder, beaked hazel, serviceberry, and mountain ash. Beeches have subtle greenish flowers, as do elms and the larger ashes, but their unspectacular beauty has yet to inspire poets or bus tours.

For their part, all the willows, poplars, birches, alders, oaks, and ironwood produce catkins as flowers, pendulous filmy growths that fill the air with pollen or clog window screens with seeds borne on silky hairs. The array and different stages of both pollen and seed catkins is staggering —sometimes found on the same tree, sometimes not— depending on the tree species.

Similarly, the pines, spruces, larches, firs, junipers, and cedars all put out flowers in the form of separate tiny pollen and seed cones, the former pollinating the latter, which later develop into the larger dry "pine cones" people more often associate with these species. So prodigious is the production of pollen from miniature pollen cones that it forms a yellow slick on quiet bays in early summer. Gliding a canoe through these cuts a neat channel of dark water and swirling dimples where my paddle has dipped. Later, spring pines produce lovely "candles"—fresh new growth standing upright at the end of every branch, decorated

by Nature like wax candles on a traditional European
Christmas tree.

Forest flowers bring new color and life to the North.
In fact, it is hard to imagine a greater transformation of the
land than occurs over just ninety days between the beginning
of a snow-bound March and the end of a verdant May. In all
of this, the artist in me sees *form*—changing line, shape and
hue; the biologist in me sees *function*—an elegantly evolved
stratagem for renewal and genetic exchange. Forest flowers
are beautiful; forest flowers ensure survival.

On Your Own Power

ONE OF MY FAVORITE spring rituals is rechristening
my canoe while there is still snow on the portages. Properly
stored during a long winter, any boat seems especially
buoyant when it first slides into lakes or rivers fresh with
meltwater. And usually an overwintering spider or two goes
along for the ride. On the first few strokes, the spring water
feels brisk on my fingertips, and it runs cold down the paddle
blade tilted up for a drink. But above all, it feels good to be
moving myself along, direct and true, on my own power.

There is an unusually evocative definition of "wilderness
parks" buried in a document titled *Ontario Provincial Parks
Planning and Management Policies*: "Large areas where the
forces of nature are permitted to function freely and where
visitors travel by non-mechanized means." I've often
wondered who exactly came up with that phrase, "travel by
non-mechanized means." What kind of discussion did it

attract behind closed bureaucratic doors, both philosophically and in more pragmatic terms, concerning what it really meant and how it would be enforced? In any case, someone bravely chose to equate respect for wilderness with modes of travel powered only by human strength, and ensconced the concept in government policy.

Snowshoeing, skiing, skating, paddling, rowing, sailing, and walking are all non-mechanized means of travel. And what do they have in common? None of them requires roads or assistance from an engine other than our own hearts, they are relatively quiet, they require some human effort, and they stand a reasonable chance of being good for you—all things that society desperately needs, yet seems bent on eliminating from most human activity.

Traveling under your own power also requires adaptation, by rolling with the elements rather than attempting to roll over them. To me, the challenge of wilderness travel has always been to make myself as comfortable as possible even under difficult circumstances, rather than boasting about the suffering I endured. Once, by telling them that "the Indians used to do it all the time," I persuaded a group I was guiding on a long canoe trip over big water that we should sleep by day and travel by night. It worked quite well, because the wind went down in the evening, which made paddling that much easier. Certainly no one suffered from sunstroke. Everyone learned to find directions using the stars. And "lunch" was simply prepared at midnight, instead of midday.

But how, exactly, do we attune ourselves to the elements and landscape while barreling through the environment by mechanized means? Particularly pernicious when they penetrate wild backcountry are all manner of "outdoor recreational vehicles," including snowmobiles, "three-wheelers," four-wheel-drive trucks, sport utility vehicles, ultra-light aircraft, balloon-tired or tracked all-terrain vehicles, trail motorcycles, and now "personal watercraft." I am not disputing the utility of some of these for work or emergency purposes. Nor am I against establishing special recreational areas, complete with moguls, tracks, hills, jumps, banked curves, straightaways, and every other possible amenity for the thrill-seeker. But I strongly believe that these things have no business simply as "recreational" vehicles in wild backcountry intended to be appreciated for its natural values.

Just how *do* you appreciate a jack-in-the-pulpit when it is being ground up under a tundra-tire? Or the fine lichen patterns on exposed rock by a lake in winter at fifty miles (80 km) per hour? Or the flutelike call of a wood thrush, through a helmet and over the whine of a 1,500-cc engine? Or a pair of loons who are no longer there because their nest has been washed out by speeding watercraft? Come to think of it, how do you appreciate just about anything, going by so quickly, especially when you need to concentrate so firmly on where you're going?

The point is that motorized travel in natural areas robs its participants of experiences they might otherwise enjoy, and spoils those same experiences for others who choose to travel quietly, unmotorized. The two don't mix. Obviously ruled out should be those cases where all-terrain vehicles do serious environmental damage, for example, compacting sensitive vegetation in the interior bogs of Newfoundland, or running over endangered piping plover nests on the beaches of Prince Edward Island. Nevertheless, some people argue, "If you don't like them, you don't have to buy one," disregarding the fact that recreational vehicles have become so ubiquitous that we all have to endure them, whether or not we choose to participate.

Unfortunately, the debate over the merits of outdoor recreational vehicles is only going to intensify. Peace and quiet, in accessible wild country, are becoming harder and harder to find; as a result there is competition between the two schools of thought for use of the same piece of ground. There will no doubt be attempts to schedule uses so that one user doesn't bump into the other, with limited success. And probably no good will be served by intolerantly arguing for or against recreational vehicles in general, because their owners tend to love them with the same intensity as those who hate them. Instead, decisions must focus on where these things will be allowed to go, and where they will not.

Outdoor recreational vehicles have become a serious environmental concern and a public policy issue not entirely foreseen by prescient conservationists such as Muir and Leopold, although Leopold in the 1940s decried "mechanized outings" as "at best a milk-and-water affair ... which has already seized nine-tenths of the woods and mountains." These early thinkers would cringe at how difficult it has become to draw a line past which these machines may not go. And I believe they would see this issue as putting our commitment to true wilderness, and to traveling through it on our own power, to a crucial test.

As for me, apart from the drive in, I choose not to travel anywhere around Loon Lake "by mechanized means." Further, I have registered a Conservation Agreement on title that will disallow them for another 999 years and be binding on all future owners of the property. This, I am told, "devalues" my land in current real estate terms, which I am pleased to trade for this small comfort: at least my small piece of Canadian wilderness will not legally experience "mechanized travel" for the next millennium, hereby decided and guaranteed on my own power.

Earth Day, April 22

IMAGES OF THIS AFTERNOON'S walk still swirl around me, rich and unforgettable. It's early evening now, I'm sitting in my cabin's screened porch overlooking Loon Lake as the Earth turns its shoulder on the Sun. It was warm enough to set out in shirtsleeves today, and to enjoy that time of year that my old friend Evan Jack used to call "after the snow and before the flies." In fact, the last of the snow and ice still stubbornly held the sheltered bottomlands, and enough insects were about to feed early fly-catching phoebes, but not yet the swallows that are due any day.

During my long hike, I startled two pairs of mated mallards, who leaped up from a beaver pond, then circled back repeatedly low overhead to investigate what I was. No duck would be so inquisitive and trusting of humans after opening day of the hunting season. (But obviously this was not September.)

A drake wood duck, iridesplendent beyond belief, lifted off the water in an unconcerned manner to put barely three more yards (10 m) between him and me, reluctant to abandon his demure but adoring hen lest a more brilliant suitor take his place. (Obviously, this was not October.)

A white-tailed doe casually took her leave, cantering but not bounding, to reappear through the bush three times in a large lazy semicircle, until she was downwind and got a snoot-full of human. (Obviously this was not November.)

A large ruffed grouse jumped up, stirring dried leaves from a wide oak savanna, waiting until I almost stepped on it before it flushed. (Obviously, this was not September, October, or November.)

A garter snake, fresh from its winter hibernaculum in the rocks, fled instinctively as I cast my shadow on its warm spot in crunchy-dry caribou moss on a sunny ridge. When I froze, trying to indicate no harm intended, it crawled back over my boot toe as if to reciprocate. Certainly if any creature could make good use of a *pax natura* with humans, it would be the much-persecuted snake. (Such a truce would also be a "giant step for mankind.")

Painted turtles basked on logs, their surprisingly long uplifted necks yearning for heat from the solar source of life. Seven of them were lined up, paying homage to their sun god like little Aztec shamans. I still puzzle over why turtles, apparently safe out in the middle of a pond, spook so easily and slide quickly away at the slightest sound or movement far away on land. (Raccoons? Otters?)

A Blanding's turtle startled, scuttled, and plopped into the water just in front of me, burrowing immediately into the still-cold mud. Because this turtle, now officially classified elsewhere in Canada as "vulnerable," lives in these ponds, the federal Canadian Wildlife Service has officially classified my property as "ecologically sensitive," which brings with it special tax benefits. Thank you, gentle turtle, but rest assured I would have protected you in any case. (Still, it's a true sign of progress when woodland turtles find as unlikely an ally as Revenue Canada.)

The very first butterflies (mourning cloaks) fluttered through gray-limbed trunks and branches, with snappy yellow trailing edges to set off their deep maroon wings. And close inspection of the dry brown forest floor revealed the very first tiny hepaticas in pale blues, pinks, purples, and whites, bravely defying a late snow. (These first dashes of color are hints of much more to come.)

A deafening "chucking" and "creaking" of tree frogs was reduced to complete silence when I approached a secluded forest meltpool. (To make me feel worse, I am certain they started up again, as soon as I left.)

Two hours into my walk, I stopped to rest for a while sitting on a rocky lookout. When I stood up, I realized that a turkey vulture exiting the crown of a nearby pine had been quietly watching me during my entire rest. (I know I was still, but not that still!)

A dapper little chipmunk eyed me warily, giving me a wide berth on its way to somewhere else. And a muskrat skulked quietly away down a marshy channel, confident it had gone unseen. (Two more reminders of Nature's apparent suspicion of humans.)

A male sapsucker found a sufficiently hollow limb to startle me by knocking out a reverberating invitation for courtship with any other of its kind within hearing distance.

A blue jay made a sound like a rusty water pump; a flicker
laughed; and a male ruffed grouse drummed his quickening
"pum ... pum ... pum ... pum, pum, pum, pum-pum-pum."
(This sound seems to be more felt than heard.)

When I returned to the cabin, "Mrs. Phoebe" flushed
from her nest in the rafter over the front stoop of my cabin.
This species of flycatcher returns as early as any to Canada.
And this particular family line has returned from points
south of Mexico to take up residence on this very spot every
spring now for thirty years. (Whenever I weatherproof
that rafter, my brush carefully leaves Mrs. Phoebe's mud-
caked home undisturbed.)

Now my boots are off, my feet are breathing, my legs
are comfortably tired and propped up to rest in the screened
porch. I watch the Sun slide slowly into a yellow-orange
watercolor wash that silhouettes a stately western skyline of
mature white pines reminiscent of the old days. If I blur my
eyes (and sharpen my imagination), I can envisage the
cathedral of 150-foot (45-m) trunks and windswept crowns
that encircled Loon Lake before the loggers took out the
straightest boles as masts for Her Majesty's navy over a
century ago. (The pines with double heads were considered
useless and therefore were spared. These rejects now serve
to remind and inspire us of what used to be, or could have
been, and might be again.)

Tonight, I share the lake with a solitary loon, restlessly
appearing, reappearing, and gazing down into every corner
of the lake. It can't have been here long, because ice still
glistened in one westerly bay this afternoon. I imagine this
loon to be waiting for its mate, though they usually arrive

together. Tonight will likely tell me whether it is truly alone, when darkness gives rise to the drawn-out, lingering "Where … are … you?" howl of this wilderness icon. (An unrequited call will mean "still waiting"; a response will mean a good chance for loon chicks again this year.)

Even by night, geese are pouring north now, drifting along on a south wind high in the fading light. There are a few days in the spring and fall when the "glurking" of geese ebbs and wanes but never stops entirely. No sooner does one strand disappear over the trees than another shows up on the opposite horizon. Normally, I can quickly locate any waving skein of Canada geese by their sound, but I cannot see these tonight. (Spring is arriving inexorably on its own, whether or not I see everything that's going on.)

Snipe are winnowing—a reedlike, accelerating "who-who-who." A woodcock calls "peent" (like a summer nighthawk), while performing its mating dance on the ground. Then he "twitters" skyward out of sight in a dramatic flight that ends in a "chortling" acrobatic dive earthward. (The whole thing will be repeated for an hour into deep dark, then again just before dawn.)

The spring peepers are tuning up. They dominate the earthy dank dusk with a cacophony of individual "peeps" that testify to millions of inch-long chorus members out there. (To be in the midst of this is to feel the physical ring in your ears, almost painful from the sheer din.)

Now a loon calls from a distant lake. Mine rushes anxiously over the water's surface with flapping wings, yodeling impatiently, expectantly. Migrating robins fuss in the upper branches of swamp-bound winterberry, after a

busy day of flipping leaves for food on the forest floor. A
lone song sparrow sends a plaintive tune out over the lake.
And a jet airliner rumbles over, barely audible at 30,000 feet
(10,000 m), but leaving its mark nevertheless—a dramatically
backlit vapor trail. Soon an otter slips quietly off the point,
gliding into and breaking up the reflection of the plane's
path, oblivious to the huge computer-guided machine
carrying three hundred people and their folding trays far
above.

In the afterglow of sunset, the lake surface now perfectly
reflects the sky, so that inverting the image of sky, treeline,
and water would produce exactly the same picture.
Reflections from Loon Lake hang there silently before me
like a surreal painting—earthbound lake and land, made
possible by their heavenly context. I'm reminded of
Shakespeare's play within a play, or dream within a dream.
Which is real, which is reflected? Which is Heaven, which
is Earth?

If there is a Heaven, then it is here on Earth simply
waiting to be noticed. Life could not have been breathed into
anything more beautiful.

Snoozing Porcupines and Soughing Pines

IN WINTER AND SPRING, when there are no other live
leaves for competition, the wind makes a soft rushing sound

through pine needles that is described by poets as "soughing," and defined by dictionaries as "a deep sigh." The bigger and thicker the pines, the deeper the sigh, which sensitively ebbs and flows with the strength of the breeze. Wind is eternally restless and elusive, always coming-from or going-to, always relying on something else to be seen, felt, or heard. Pine boughs mark its passing with a sigh.

As a boy, I used to enjoy climbing old white pines and sitting right up there in the crowns themselves for a "total-surround" soughing experience. One spring, I discovered a clutch of great horned owlets in the top of such a tree, and in between the hisses and dive-bombs of their parents, I snapped pictures of the young birds with, appropriately, my Brownie "Hawkeye" camera. At times like that I could hear exactly what soothed a nest of owls, or a snoozing porcupine on a sunny spring day. In fact, I now believe that although the rest of us may enjoy soughing pines vicariously, this tune is really a lasting lullaby composed first and foremost for *Erethizon dorsatum*—the "animal with the irritating back." No doubt the Creator foresaw that the porcupine deserved and would need its own melody, as consolation for the many myths that would inevitably grow up around it. Here are ten:

1 *Porcupines throw their quills.* Wrong. Porcupines release their quills on contact by an attacker, especially with a whiplike swat of their spiny tails.

2 *Porcupine quills are poisonous.* Wrong. Researchers report that in fact they contain a fatty acid that serves as an antibiotic, which explains why anything stuck by a porcupine rarely develops an infection.

3 *Porcupines, unless shot or pushed, never fall out of trees.*
Wrong. One study indicated that nine out of fifteen
adult porcupines had broken bones from falls.

4 *Porcupines never get stabbed by their own quills.* Wrong.
This likely does happen when they fall out of trees!

5 *Porcupines can't run.* Wrong. On many occasions, I have
personally watched them lift their bodies up clear of the
ground, and clip along at a brisk pace on all fours.

6 *Porcupines are like pigs, because they foul their own nest.*
Wrong. Porcupines (unlike animals such as raccoons
that have a reused latrine) actually defecate and urinate
wherever they happen to be. This explains why urine
stains are commonly found in their winter trails, or
among scats scattered among their buds and clippings
on the forest floor. Porcupines "go as they go." However,
it is true that huge piles of droppings accumulate in the
bottom of hollow den trees, or rock piles where
porcupines spend prolonged periods in winter.

7 *Porcupines have no voice.* Wrong. Although porcupines
are solitary and relatively peaceful creatures, they have
a remarkable repertoire of squeals, grunts, bleats, snorts,
barks, screams, cries, hums, and moans. I once a heard
a Manitoba wildlife biologist granted a national radio
audience on the CBC because he knew porcupines well
enough to imitate them. Nice lesson for the nation; I
hope we were listening.

8 *Porcupines can't mate.* Obviously wrong, or they would
have vanished as a species long ago. Nevertheless, mating
does appear to be a dicey exercise, and researchers don't
always agree on how it occurs.

A.W. F. Banfield, for example, in *Mammals of Canada*, describes a "comical roughhouse sort of dance. They rise on their hind feet and dance toward each other, whining and grunting. They may place their paws on each other's shoulders and rub noses; then they cuff each other affectionately on the head and usually bowl one another with blows and shoves." Other researchers report that, at the moment of truth, the female elevates her tail up over her back to accommodate the male's quill-less belly, which makes sense for both parties.

9 *Porcupines can't give birth, at least not comfortably.* Wrong. In fact, new-born porcupines (usually only one per female) are born with their quills soft, wet, flat, and limp. However, the young are reported to be able to climb trees in less than a day. And Banfield says, "Soon after birth, young porcupines displayed the instinctive behavior pattern of backing into a proffered hand. They will also follow anyone who moves away from them, and rub against one's face if he whines. In marked contrast to their stolid elders, they are very playful." If anyone would like to experiment and verify this information, I'd be pleased to hear of the results.

10 *Porcupines are good for nothing.* Also wrong. This is often a forester speaking, because porcupines can damage standing timber by stripping the bark and cambium, beginning with the upper limbs and moving down the trunk. Further, their metabolic need for salt leads porcupines to eat virtually anything wooden which is impregnated with perspiration, including ax handles, paddles, canoe gunwales, and outhouse seats. I can report that this applies as well to the glues or resins in plywood.

Porcupines' salt-need also draws them to road-salt, where they become road-kills.

However, in answer to the question, "What good *is* a porcupine?" consider the following additional ten points:

1 *Porcupines are sluggish enough to be easily captured for food if you are lost or starving in the bush.* I was told this repeatedly by Ojibway schoolmates and elders in northern Ontario, where I was raised, and Banfield reports "knowing of one Royal Canadian Mounted policeman who owes his life to the discovery of a porcupine in the last trees on the edge of the tundra zone of the Northwest Territories." Samuel Hearne, the eighteenth-century explorer, reported that Indian guides would note the location of porcupines, knowing they wouldn't venture far from where they were spotted in winter, so they could be taken for food on the return trip if necessary.

2 *By girdling some trees and creating dead limbs, porcupines provide homes for cavity-nesting birds and mammals, and invading insect food for them as well.* Furthermore, if it's only the tops of trees that are girdled and reduced to "stagheads," or if only the leaders are taken, creating many stems, no real harm is done to the trees—from Nature's standpoint at least, though perhaps not an industrial forester's.

3 *Porcupines are a preferred food for fishers, which have learned how to kill them without getting spiked.* Fishers have become rare in many parts of Ontario, to the point of now being reintroduced. In the 1960s at Loon Lake, porcupines were everywhere. I could look out from a

hillside in April and easily spot half a dozen. But fishers were nowhere to be found. Now there are fewer porcupines, and coincidentally a local resident working his trapline on Crown land to the north reports a good catch of fishers every winter. Today, I'm pleased to have both natural predator and prey on my land.

4 *Porcupine quills have been used by Aboriginal peoples for making beautiful embroidered decorative work on moccasins, belts, bags, and jewelry.* This work was so valued, it was traded between Indian bands and nations before the arrival of Europeans. It is still sold for important community income as a high-quality Canadian craft item.

5 *Porcupines, by feeding on different tree species at different times of the year—aspen and sugar maple buds in the spring; basswood, beech, ash, yellow birch in the summer; oak acorns, pine, and hemlock in the fall; and virtually all of these in winter—are in fact helping to maintain some natural diversity in our forests.* Besides, they don't just munch on trees. Porcupines also feed on plants such as raspberry canes, mushrooms, and water lilies (their air-filled quills make them especially buoyant swimmers). In 1989, I found one out in the open of the Khutzeymateen River estuary in northern British Columbia feeding on sedges.

6 *Porcupines nip off tender buds and growth, such as sugar maple and pine shoots, which fall to the forest floor and are subsequently eaten by other animals such as deer.* The great mammologist and wildlife observer Olaus Murie recounts, "One evening when making camp I found a great quantity of porcupine twigs around the base of a

tree, enough to make a comfortable bed on which to spread my sleeping bag."

7   *Porcupines are fascinating, in and of themselves, and provide unique evidence of our evolutionary past.* Absolutely true. Our porcupines are the only representatives of a New World family of porcupines that traversed Central America from South America during the Pleistocene era, to evolve as a completely separate family from the Old World porcupine species. What else do we have that even remotely resembles a porcupine in North America?

8   *Porcupines are good company.* When other mammals are hibernating or refusing to venture forth in winter and early spring, chances are a porcupine will be out feeding at night or dozing during the day.

9   *Most animals, through one bad experience, learn not to fool with porcupines.* My first Labrador retriever, Walter, managed to get quills in his lips, tongue, throat, cheek, neck, and shoulder—all in one encounter. Although I thought I had removed all the quills with pliers (and a yelp), because of their tiny barbs a number migrated through his body and emerged from the base of his tail four months later. Walter left porcupines alone thereafter. A senior scientist studying foxes for the Ontario Ministry of Natural Resources tells me he almost never finds a rabid fox without quills in its face, perhaps a measure of the poor animal's dementia. Farmers report the same for rabid cows. So, the porcupine has inadvertently provided us with a possible test to recognize and avoid rabies-infected animals.

10   I give the tenth point in favor of porcupines to Paul
     Renzendes, a researcher who has discovered that
     porcupines eat false truffles. Here is Renzendes' own
     account of ecological elegance brought about by the
     lowly "pig of the pines":

     If we are paying attention, nature has many ways of
     showing us how things are connected. The truffle attaches
     itself to the root of the hemlock and sends out its own
     roots. These roots are much more efficient than hemlock
     roots at picking up minerals and water, and they end up
     feeding the hemlock, allowing it to grow more vigorously.
     The hemlock, in turn, gives sugars to the mushroom
     that the mushroom can't produce. Then the mushroom
     sends out this fruiting body, which emits a scent that
     attracts the porcupine. The porcupine comes and eats it,
     the spores go into the porcupine's intestinal tract, and
     when the porcupine defecates, it sows the spores. The
     porcupine feeds on the hemlock, but also gives
     something back.

Finally, the clincher. If not for the porcupine, we might not
have been blessed with soughing pines.

On Patience

TODAY I HIKED UP to a small isolated lake on nearby
Crown land, permanently cottage-less, and simply sat there
quietly for an hour to see what I could see.

I suppose this was an act of patience in its own right, but it was richly rewarded. Among other things, a great blue heron sailed in on a tailwind, totally unaware of my presence, and wheeled 180 degrees to land upwind on top of a drowned, broken spruce with barely a dozen gray limbs left for a crown.

The bird gracefully carried a yard-long forked stick in its beak, and immediately began to adjust it into position for the beginnings of a nest. I watched this through binoculars for fully thirty minutes, careful not to move, as I was nearby and in full view on a rocky outcrop.

The heron placed and replaced that stick repeatedly. Maneuvering such a long object was a feat in itself, because it kept getting hung up at awkward angles in one branch or another. After many tries, the stick was jammed in sufficiently that the heron could let it go, but it lay more vertical than flat. So the bird patiently regrasped the stick, lifted it entirely free, and started all over again. Ten minutes later, the stick was beginning to lie more or less flat, so an end to all this was in sight.

No sooner was I convinced that the heron was finally satisfied than it would step up or down onto an adjacent limb, pick the stick up all over again, and calmly adjust it some more. There was no sense of frustration on the heron's part, but watching this mini-drama was certainly beginning to get to *me!*

I ran through some quick mental calculations as to how long it would take this bird to finish its nest at this rate— probably a month after the eggs had been laid. I found myself hoping the heron would show some sign of accomplishment, depart for another stick, and get on with it. By now, my arms were aching from holding my binoculars up, and I was stiff from making such a sustained effort not to move.

Finally, the heron had its stick more or less level. It extended its neck and head straight upward, bulged its throat feathers, and uttered some gurgling sounds that I interpreted as some version of "There, now it's time to find another one." Then my friend once again picked up the stick, which slipped out of its beak and fell down into the water below.

For an eternity, the heron stood there motionless, just cocking its head sideways occasionally, as if trying to figure out what had happened. "After all this effort," I thought, "you could at least cast a wistful glance down toward the lost stick. Or better yet, retrieve the thing!" But instead, in a very unhurried manner, the heron gently lofted itself downwind and methodically flapped away, presumably to find some more nesting material.

I was as interested in my own reaction to all of this. The learning point, for me, was not that I had totally wasted thirty minutes, or that I had witnessed a particularly stupid individual bird destined for extinction. No doubt, when I return later this year, either the great blue heron will have, for good reasons, abandoned this particular site for its nest, or there will be an elegant and perfectly adequate structure there to bring young herons into the world.

No, the lesson seemed to be that we humans cannot rush or "neaten up" Nature, except in a very limited way, no matter how much we might wish to do so. Instead, we might consider why some things take the time and assume the shape they do in a natural setting. My own profession, forestry, is a case in point. At our best, we foresters take our tips from Nature, beginning by understanding the biological requirements of the individual tree species we are dealing with. Further, we are supposed to base stand management on replicating natural disturbances such as fire, windthrow, and other ecological processes that influence the forest at a landscape level. There's a good rule of thumb for all foresters: to the extent that we base forest management on Nature's model, we are likely practicing pretty good forestry; to the extent that we depart from this, we're likely getting into trouble. Big trouble.

It goes without saying that we can't base anything on Nature's example if we haven't set aside representative samples of natural landscapes, or allowed them to change over time under natural conditions, or taken the time to study and understand them. But for us, it seems to wait and learn is to waste time. In my view, professional foresters who arrogantly rush to make large-scale interventions into ecosystems weren't paying attention during their biology lectures. They should slow down and spend an afternoon watching herons.

If impatience is a dangerous trait in foresters, it is even more inexcusable in wildlife professionals. Consider, for example, the inclination to control predator numbers, such as wolves, in order to maintain more abundant prey species for humans to hunt, such as deer, moose, and caribou. Large-scale predator control is based on a human refusal to hunt side by side with the wolf, to experience lean years along with the good as prey numbers fluctuate under natural conditions. Instead, for us every year must be a good year. In effect, this practice says, "What Nature provides is not good enough. It must be 'enhanced.' We must speed things up." So wildlife "managers" intervene to iron out natural population peaks and troughs, seeking to maintain an artificially high prey population. These interventions in turn trigger other problems, for example, eruptions of prey numbers; poor nutrition; or overbrowsing of habitat, which degrades it for other wildlife species. Soon, and predictably, we become "hooked on management," continually having to escalate what we do in order to address problems and imbalances of our own making—problems that originated with impatience. In fact, no one manages wildlife; we can only manage ourselves, and therefore our impact on it. But managing ourselves, has proven to be much more difficult than managing anything else.

Well, that clumsy heron will manage. And so will its species, if we protect its habitat. Tapping into just thirty minutes of one bird's life, among millions, may tell us something important, not about the bird, but about ourselves.

Are we listening?

Morning Coffee on the front Stoop

IF YOU LIKE MORNING, and coffee with it, provide yourself with a sheltered place facing east. The warmth of an early sun, and the warmth of a fresh cup of coffee, were made for each other.

The front of my cabin on Loon Lake provides just such a spot, facing southeast, comfortably out of the prevailing

northwest wind. It's a "stoop," or small low step-up
entrance deck, flanked on both sides by curing firewood.
From here I can use the closed front door of my cabin as
a backrest, and greet the dawn in a manner that befits a
new day.

From here I have shooed away porcupines hoping to
gnaw my stoop. I have fed chipmunks peanuts from my hand.
I have watched Venus get overtaken by the rising Sun. I have
watched Mrs. Phoebe sit impatiently a few yards away in a
white ash sapling, waiting for me to leave, then grudgingly
return to her nest in the rafters above. I have seen ruffed
grouse pecking up sandy gravel for their gizzards. I have
welcomed three cottontail rabbits at a time, feeding on the
sweet clover that grows in front of the cabin, especially
attracted when I have scythed a few plants the evening before,
so that the heavy fragrance drifted out beckoning on the
damp air overnight. I have seen crows dive-bombing a great
horned owl (also a leftover from the dark hours), knowing
that the owl will take its revenge when night falls again. I
have heard thousands of geese moving north in the spring,
south in the fall—obviously up early in the day because
already they were mere wavering dots among the clouds. I
have been chided by a cocky house wren, thanklessly using
the house with a diminutive hole that I provided nearby, and
I confess to having pruned a modest gap through the trees
just so that I could take in such antics at this time of day. Most
important, it is from here that I have seriously studied the
morning sky, using every hard-earned bit of wisdom and
experience in me to predict what the weather has in store for
the coming day. That's usually a two-coffee exercise, with a
fifty percent chance of being wrong.

A front stoop facing east to begin the day (and a screened porch facing west for sunsets to end it)—I highly recommend both to anyone with a modest dream, and blueprints.

Renewal

SPRING IS A TIME OF RENEWAL. Some of spring's new life has lain dormant waiting to be awakened by longer days and warmer temperatures; some of it flows back in from the South that provided respite from winter.

A quickening is felt everywhere—in the trickle of melting snow now pocked into granules, in subdividing cells forming everything from new leaves to new bears, in the territorial skirmishes of chipmunks, and in the searching night call of a loon trying to locate its mate. Now our part of the Earth slowly leans closer to the source of all life— the Sun.

Spring is also irresistible. For whose heart has not been given a lift by this season, regardless of what else ails us? If winter gives us a chance to be alone, then spring brings us the company we also need. All living things get caught up in that elemental spark needed to move us from a period of rest to a period of growth.

But as welcome and necessary as it may be, the spark of new life by itself is not enough. Spring offers a promise; summer determines whether that promise will be kept.

Summer

The Spirit of the Loon

A Pulse That Hums

Fishing

Hummingbirds and Cardinal Flowers

Summer Deer in Jewelweed

Night Freights

Early-Morning Paddle

Summer Storm

Evening Song

Growth

The Spirit of the Loon

People familiar with loons get the loon inside them,
like a totem, and it seems to make a little dark gap in the
smooth base of rationality we try to keep for our thoughts.
Joan Dunning, from *The Loon: Voice of the Wilderness*

IN HER EXCELLENT, self-illustrated book on loons, Joan Dunning not only documents the annual life cycle of a bird, but also evokes the mystique of a wilderness icon. What a wonderful literary accomplishment, because it is the *spirit* more than the biology of the loon that moves us.

That spirit rides on that voice, which sings of wilderness. In my case, it helps that Loon Lake was shaped first by the glaciers, and later by surrounding pines, as a superb outdoor concert hall, configured acoustically by Nature to provide perfect reverberation for its namesake's call. If you have loons on your lake, then it must harbor wild haunts of solitude, because loons just will not thrive anywhere else. They offer humanity a breathtaking bargain: "If you want us and our voice, then leave some things wild." Such a modest request. Such an overwhelming benefit for humanity. Yet we are increasingly unable to deliver on our part of the contract.

The spirit of the loon bobs, newly arrived, off the April ice edge in my lake. It roils and spatters in skittering runs along the surface during breeding season, and quietly searches the shoreline for makeshift nest material. It hides motionless and silent while hatching young near the water's edge, then appears in summer riding lightly on a parent's back as a charcoal ball of fluff. The spirit of the loon flashes on checkered wings being stretched or folded in the afternoon sun, and circles the lake, laboring to gain enough altitude to clear the trees. It dives sleekly into cold pockets, and leaves swirls of warm black mud in shallow bays, exchanging fish life for loon life. It departs with the parents shortly after duck season opens, then lingers as a lone young bird which bravely heads south at freeze-up. And always, the spirit of the loon is there in that voice, in the yearning wail to locate a mate at night, in the nervous tremolo when a canoe or fox approaches too close, in the male's aggressive yodel to defend his family's home, and in the friendly little hoots and barks of informal loon chit-chat.

The first time I ever heard a loon wail, I was a small boy visiting a friend's cottage, and I thought it might be a wolf. It could just as well have been. Because what we feel in both the howl of a wolf and the call of a loon is pure wildness. Aldo Leopold's life was transformed by watching the green fire in the emerald eye of a wolf die; ours must never be transformed by killing the burning round ruby in the eye of the loon.

A Pulse That Hums

IF AN EXPERIENCED eye can accurately guess the time of year based on seeing a square yard of the forest floor around Loon Lake, then a well-tuned ear could do the same by listening for a minute to which insects are out and about.

Summer, in particular, moves along in discrete stages that are synchronized to the background music of various bugs, beetles, and biting flies.

Early summer (June) is characterized by leftovers from spring, especially blackflies that really had their day in May. These little biters hatched the preceding fall and overwintered under the ice to spin cocoons and emerge in the spring through a bubble that brings the adult blackfly to the surface. Spring hordes die off through desiccation after a few hot days in a row, but subsequent broods develop as larvae in fast-running water. So, a few cloudy days in June and July can bring on unwelcome new generations. Blackflies hover annoyingly around your face, but seem to take their preferred pound of flesh from the nape of your neck or from tender skin behind your ears. Anything this plentiful, it can be safely assumed, has an important ecological purpose. Sure enough, blackflies are crucial to tiding over early migratory birds, and they also pollinate many plants, for example, blueberries. For that sweet berry of August we are indebted to those nasty pests of May.

Mosquitoes also rely on meltpools and a rainy spring to reach peak numbers in June. Their activity is "keyed to light levels," which in plain language means they are out in force at daybreak and dusk. At Loon Lake, summer mosquitoes are worst just when the bass fishing is best. If I put my hand on the inside of a screen window at dusk, mosquitoes can be sufficiently attracted by my breath and the warmth of my skin to form a perfect black silhouette of my hand when I pull it away. Biting flies in these numbers create an inescapable ambient whining din at night that resonates with life everywhere. So mosquitoes make summer a good time to be out on the water, or camping on a breezy point, but not deep in the bush. I find the best defense to be a number of days without a bath until I smell something like an old bear, and then to simply accept mosquitoes as a fact of life rather than fretting over every little whine and bite.

As with blackflies, mosquitoes serve a useful purpose as food for fish, birds, and amphibians. But perhaps none of their predators is as well known as the dragonfly—especially the whitetail, with its bright white abdomen and black bands on its wings, and the green darner, with iridescent lime-colored body and purple abdomen. Dragonflies at rest hold their wings out stiffly to the side and have been described as "helicopter gunships" coming to our rescue by eating millions of insects that would otherwise torment humans. Beautiful damselflies provide the same service, but they hold their translucent fishnet wings together up over long slender bodies that resemble batons painted with neat vertical bands of sky blue and jet black.

Early summer along streams and beaver ponds at Loon Lake also brings forth misty swarms of mating midges, short-lived mayflies much loved by trout, craneflies tapping at night on a window lit from inside my cabin, and long stoneflies that crawl rather than fly away from anything perceived as a threat. Meanwhile, the deep woods flutter with large mourning-cloak butterflies; little tan wood satyrs with black "eye spots"; and smaller, bright blue, spring azures, which rely on new dogwood and blueberry leaves for food.

On the pathogen front, tent caterpillars begin wriggling by the hundreds inside their silken hammocks hung from black cherry trees, then leave the trees to pupate and emerge as bland brown moths. Watch for black-billed cuckoos in summer to help keep them in check. Also, since I refuse to spray pesticides, it was at this time of year in 1972 that I obtained by mail, in a vial, a virus from the Great Lakes Forest Experiment Station, and released it as a successful biological control for red-headed pine saw flies to help protect Evan's planted trees. In the 1980s, early summer was the time of year when larval gypsy moths appeared everywhere and ate three-quarters of the foliage they would consume in their entire life cycle, defoliating over fifty percent of my oaks.

Midsummer (July) is ushered in by June bugs, perfectly described in a National Audubon guide as "flying clumsily about, slamming into window screens, noisily colliding with outdoor lights, ricocheting off porch walls and clattering across the floor." From my own screened porch, I see the first male fireflies, glowing, gliding, flickering, and blinking at night in the greenery down by the lake. Sometimes I track one in particular and try to guess where it will reappear when it lights up. The flightless females answer from secret places in the alders, willows, and wintergreen bushes that line Loon Lake. Recent research at Cornell indicates that some female fireflies attract mates only to eat them, thus absorbing from the males a defensive chemical that repels firefly predators such as birds, bats, and spiders.

If I am lucky, my screen will also be paid a quiet night visit by the lovely luna moth, a pale green giant the size of a small bird, with two striking eye spots and long graceful tails sweeping back from its hind wings. However, look for lunas only where pesticides are absent, as they are particularly susceptible to these biocides.

Midsummer insect activity focuses intensively on the water—whirligig beetles mill about like "flotillas of watermelon seeds," water boatmen and backswimmers row their way to and fro with oarlike legs, and water striders utilize surface tension to scoot across the top of the lake.

The transition to late summer is marked by the unwelcome arrival of deer- and horseflies. These big buzzing chompers hover and tick against my old straw hat as I walk along sunny ridges or stand in the open to unlock my roadside gate. One local real estate agent automatically breaks off a branch of leaves to use as a switch when showing bush properties in summer. There's nothing subtle about the bite of a deerfly or horsefly. It hurts. And by the time you first feel the tickle of the fly, swat as you may, it is likely too late to do anything about it, because you will have been already bitten.

In late summer (August), cicadas loudly whine away dull, hot afternoons. Adult cicadas look like two-inch (5-cm) giant green houseflies, and the familiar dog-day buzzing is produced by males vibrating membranes at the base of their stomachs. This species can spend as long as seventeen years underground in the nymph stage! So think of the cicada's "song" as an expression of sheer joy on being released from the cloistered damp dark earth into the unbounded warmth and bright sun of August.

Now the *Tyrannosaurus rex* of the insect world, the praying mantis, matures and sets about its hunt. Long green and tan adults with front legs folded under their

powerful jaws lurk in straw-colored late-season grass.
Field crickets tune up and chirp confidently all evening,
right into the cold weather of fall. Grasshoppers exude a
lulling trill and kick up in front of anyone walking through
old fields or grassy woodland openings, while road dusters
fly clickity-clacking away from oncoming cars and walkers
on backcountry gravel roads. Sometimes they race
groundhogs ducking for cover off road shoulders. And now
the first monarch butterflies head south, the last generation
raised in the North that will overwinter in Mexico, to be
succeeded by the several generations it takes to march
north next spring. So that truly *is* the last we will ever see
of that lonely individual monarch fluttering southward
in August.

Probably seventy percent of all animal species on Earth
are insects, most of them unnamed. No wonder, then, that
the season when insects are most active in Canada—summer
—can be conveniently measured by their comings and
goings. In my cabin at Loon Lake, cluster flies first stir in
early spring on windowsills where the sun's warmth is
magnified and trapped by glass panes. Then they are liberated
by summer, slowed by fall, and sent back into a torpor by the
first frosts and snows of winter. Thus, common flies serve as
brackets for a burst of seasonal activity by thousands of other
insect species that anchor the northern food chain. In fact,
without insects our entire global ecosystem would collapse.
It is fitting, therefore, that their chirps, hums, whirrs, buzzes,
whines, flutters—and yes, their bites and stings—have
worked their way into our unconscious experience of the
seasons and the world itself.

Fishing

ON FRIDAY AFTERNOONS in June, a gentle beckoning
sifted in on the wind through the windows of the makeshift,
portable school I attended as a boy in northern Ontario.
Grades five to thirteen were all crammed into one classroom
—the children of laborers, foremen, heavy-equipment
operators, engineers, and supervisory staff from a hydro
camp, along with Ojibway kids from the White Dog Reserve.
No matter what our background, virtually all of us were
restless to get out of that place and go fishing.

During afternoon recess, details were planned regarding
who was going to fish where, most of it bluff or subterfuge
in order to keep exact locations a secret. In any case, the rest
of the school day was a total write-off as far as schoolwork
was concerned. And I remember busting out of those doors
at 3:20 p.m. like Davy Crockett in the movie, charging into
the U.S. Congress. Once, my teacher shrieked at me, "Get
back in here and leave properly!" But it was too late—I was
long gone, with my honey-colored spaniel, Roxy, not far
behind.

Now, grown-ups sport bumper stickers that claim "I'd
rather be fishing" or "The worst day of fishing beats the
best day at work." On the one hand, this deep-seated
yearning to be doing something else reminds us that most
people don't really enjoy their job very much. On the other
hand, it's obviously meant to evoke what Ontario sportsman
and author Tiny Bennett simply called "the joy of fishing."
Even Aldo Leopold claimed, "Prudence is entirely absent

from fishing as a way of wasting weekends ... in direct contrast to the experiences of the workaday life."

In my case, I know that one of the most thrilling days of my life was as a ten-year-old, when my father replaced my cheap, broken old bait-casting reel and steel rod with a brand new spincast outfit (based on his winnings from a poker game in Kenora). But the water I fished as a boy—the English River—was tragically to become contaminated by mercury from an upstream chloralkali plant associated with the pulp and paper industry. I returned ten years after those halcyon school days to find "Fish for Fun Only" signs posted up and down my river by the provincial government, which message appeared against the screened image of a skull and cross-bones. Those fish were no longer fit to eat and had to be thrown back. And the Ojibway kids I went to school with had lost a commercial fishery, as well as jobs guiding sport anglers; social, economic, and personal depression came down on their already poor community like a sledgehammer. For them, fishing was more than a happy meditation or discretionary hobby. It was a way of life, and it was taken away by forces beyond their control. What happened to my home river, and to the people who depended on it, did more to propel me into a career of environmentalism than any other single event in my life.

Of course, fishing also has its detractors. Some people argue that it is cruel. Some can accept fishing for subsistence purposes, but not for "sport." Others have problems with certain fishing practices—legal, illegal, or high-tech— which they consider unethical. Whatever your view on these matters, it is clear that any practice that is biologically unsustainable is wrong for both fish and people (which unfortunately accounts for about seventy-five percent of the commercial fisheries in the world today).

For my part, I have threaded my way through this moral labyrinth by following a few simple rules: I no longer use live bait; I rely on my knowledge of the waters rather than electronic fish-finding gadgets; and I keep only what I plan to eat for my next meal. Having made these concessions, I have no compunction whatsoever in joining the osprey for an evening's fishing on Loon Lake.

I've always been a good fisherman. There's a knack to it, and frankly I've got it. As a boy at White Dog Falls I earned pocket money showing people where to fish. Then for an extra twenty-five cents I'd fillet anything they caught—a skill my mother taught me as soon as I could safely sharpen a knife, because she realized it was going to save her a lot of work in the long run. Today, I'm still that irritating person in the boat who catches fish when no one else does. I just have a feeling for where the fish are—on the windward side of that shoal, over or beside that weed bed, or in the slick or eddy behind that big boulder out there in whitewater. Today's television fishing shows embellish this common sense in technospeak such as "reading structure," and they promote all manner of electronic gizmos to help with the job. But I confess to a more old-fashioned approach, and still enjoy throwing a line in where I don't know exactly what's going to happen. In my view, fishing is an art, with the unpredictable and creative element that distinguishes art from science. Success should never be assured, but rather a way of confirming whether your best guesses were right.

Perhaps most important, fishing teaches a person when to remain patient and stay at it, versus when to move on because no amount of effort is going to improve the situation—judgments that serve us well for many things in life.

A number of particularly vivid fishing experiences have served as rites of passage in my life. I remember falling asleep in my orange life jacket under the short deck of my uncle's cedar strip car-topper, with a noisy old green ten-horse Johnson pushing us down Wadsworth Lake in Ontario. I could not have been more than three or four years old. The combined fragrance of freshwater, gas, and exhaust, along with the bass and walleye scales on the floorboards, was ambrosia to me. I remember how black and deep the water looked to a non-swimmer out beyond the gunwales, how incredibly fast the boat seemed to plane along, how uniformly the water peeled out off both sides of the bow under the splashboards, and how symmetrical were the furrow and wake carved neatly out into the lake behind the transom. We would stop at secret places, drop anchor, bait hooks, and catch fish that flashed green-yellow-white as they fought their way up from below.

My uncle also took me smelt fishing at night in Lake Ontario. We built a fire on the beach and, using a small seine, filled a bushel basket with hundreds of fresh tiny shimmering silver fish. Then we cleaned, fried, and ate them for breakfast —backbones, crispy tails, and all—with salt, pepper, fresh lemon, and tartar sauce.

Later, another uncle taught me how to catch gold-eyes in the Saskatchewan River, using only butcher cord and a willow stick jammed into the bank. We tied an apple-sized

rock to one end of about twenty yards of butcher cord,
baited a half-dozen drop hooks with bits of beef, whirled the
rock and bait hooks out into the current, then positioned a
small "rider" made from a willow crotch on the taut line.
When the telltale rider started bouncing madly, you knew
you had one on the line (sometimes two), and we towed
the fish in hand over hand, rebaited the hook, then tossed
the whole outfit back out into the river. My cousin and I
manned half a dozen lines each, and usually caught enough
fish to feed the entire family and few hired men back on
the farm. My only fear was that someday from those muddy
depths we'd accidentally catch a huge sturgeon, which I
was told were "so big their tails flop out the back of a
hay wagon."

One summer evening when I was fifteen, I was fishing
for bass in Georgian Bay from a canoe. I was using a tiny,
red-and-white daredevil spinning spoon, with a single treble
hook more suitable for brook trout, and six-pound test line
—not exactly the gear one would choose to tie into a thirty-
pound (14-kg) muskellunge! That fish towed the canoe up
and down channels past many islands over a two-hour period,
and was so heavy it went right through one landing net
(through which I had to thread my rod and reel with the fish
still on). The muskellunge was much longer than the canoe
was wide, so I was preparing to go ashore to beach it when
a large motor boat was summoned, from which I finally
landed the fish just as the sun set. Catching a legendary
"muskie" was a lifetime dream for me in those days, and
since I had the money—I'd been saving up for something
else—I proudly decided to have the fish mounted. Interesting,

because as I look at it on the wall today, I'm reasonably sure that muskie was a large female, and these days I would never consider even keeping it, let alone getting it "stuffed." Now she stares back at me as a mute reminder of a different way of thinking.

In my twenties, I double-portaged into an unnamed lake near Quetico Park one day with a woodsman friend who moved through the bush faster than any person I have known. Since he carried virtually nothing, I was astonished at how everything from tea bags to a forty-eight-ounce juice tin, a frying pan, even a cached canoe, kept appearing just when we needed them, along with our limit in fresh, eating-size walleye. A very wise handyman at Quetico Centre taught me how to catch spring lake trout from Eva Lake using a set-line by casting a baitfish out, then letting it drop down deep to the bottom of the lake. He prepared those fresh trout in a smokehouse that he had custom-built, using firewood he cut especially for the job and a recipe I have racked my brains to remember.

My work with World Wildlife Fund has caused me to happily cross paths with fishes and aquafauna of all descriptions. For example, I waded the Grand River of Ontario, now a Canadian Heritage River, in search of the three-inch (7-cm) silver-shiner—a stream species thought to be disappearing from those waters. Ironically, during my interviews for the job as head of WWF Canada, my activist background was a controversial factor: two members of the board threatened to resign if I was hired, while two threatened to resign if I wasn't. One of my detractors asked me if I was "the kind of person who would stop a

billion-dollar project just to save a stupid little three-inch fish"
(a poorly disguised reference to the renowned snail darter
that halted a large Tennessee Valley Authority project). When
I said, "Yes, if no other accommodation could be reached to
save the fish," he had all the information he needed to cast
his vote "No!" However, I got the job.

In the 1980s, I gathered small delicious mussels at low
tide near Churchill on Hudson Bay with an international
polar bear expert. In the midst of his fatherly remarks about
how we should be constantly vigilant regarding these bears,
we looked up to spot a full-grown female bear in a straight
line between us and our vehicle, with the tide coming *in*! In
the end, we not only ate the mussels, we darted and tagged
the bear.

In 1987, my WWF colleagues and I liberated our
international president, Prince Philip, from the tedium of
receiving official delegations in the upper reaches of the
Sheraton Hotel during the Commonwealth Conference in
Vancouver, to go killer-whale watching on the Inside
Passage. With volunteer help from an army of scouts, we
quickly located a resident pod of orcas, then cut the engine
for an entire afternoon to drift quietly in the sun with the
current and the whales. They were fishing and feeding on
salmon in the ocean, while we munched on a picnic lunch of
salmon sandwiches up on deck. The next day His Royal
Highness stood out at the head table, sporting a rugged tan,
while he urged a thousand business people at the Vancouver
Board of Trade to help protect the salmon and grizzlies of
the Khutzeymateen Valley. Of course, salmon was served
for lunch.

Later, to close the circle, I was fortunate enough to catch a large coho in the Khutzeymateen River myself, with the help of my young son, Doug. It was late summer, so the grizzlies were also fishing everywhere and the salmon were running. I can still feel the surprising power of that fish, hooked, but nevertheless cruising effortlessly upstream. It was hard to believe that something so beautifully animate and strong was destined to become a spent force within weeks. (Happily, forests of the Khutzeymateen were eventually protected in 1994 as Canada's first grizzly bear reserve, and Prince Philip personally celebrated the event at the invitation of the T'simshian people who have always known of the area's value as something other than feedstock for an industrial mill.)

Sherry and I collected wonderful fresh mussels in Bonavista Bay, Newfoundland, near Terra Nova National Park and site of a proposed marine protected area. We stayed in an old net-mending hut called the "Twine Loft" at Happy Adventure Cove during the height of the June capelin fishery. From our cozy perch right over the water, we watched mounded bargefuls of silver "he's" being towed out, then dumped and wasted at sea; only the "she's," with their eggs so sought after by a Japanese market, were kept. On that trip, a whale-rescuer showed us how to jig for cod, but by then it was easier to locate whales than cod.

Finally, I remember Archie Walker's broad smile as he showed me how to clean a catfish with one snap of his thumb, and how he laughed kindly when, for all my university learning, I could never quite get it right—a good example of Mark Twain's warning to "Never let your schooling interfere with your education." Francis used to catch a boatload of panfish to feed to the pigs, but the Walkers always kept the best—the "bullheads"—for themselves. One of the finest breakfasts Sherry and I ever enjoyed was a mess of fresh catfish in the cabin with Francis and his friends, and just this summer he gave me a nice sealer jar of pickled perch from Loon Lake, from the supply he keeps stored in the root cellar beneath his farmhouse.

Just another string of sentimental fishing stories? If so I apologize, but I've spared you many more! For me, these experiences serve as personal milestones marking a life path. And I hope many more lie ahead—many more beautifully spotted trout lying on a bed of fresh grass in my wicker creel. Fishing and the stories it generates are an opportunity to experience Canada first-hand. Because getting out into and onto the water; gently taking in the shoreline, the hills, the smells, and the birdsong; feeling the weather on your face as you wet a line and the current throbbing against your waders; and tasting the land during a shore-lunch— all of this is still not a bad way to get to know your country.

Now I cast into quiet bays in the evening on Loon Lake. The summer afternoon breeze has died down, and there's a restful lull before the mosquitoes become insufferable at sundown. Every yard of this shoreline is well known to me—a broken tangle of beaver lodges and food piles, deadfalls, alder thickets, and granite outcrops—the perfect backdrop for largemouth bass. Arrowhead, pickerelweed, and water lilies march out in random patterns toward my canoe. Casting here is a very precise matter of dropping a surface lure on the water just off a log to imitate a frog hopping in, or hitting small openings in the lily pads, or moving a shallow-running bait right up against, through, but not into the weeds. This is where the fish are, so getting there is the first step. Getting the fish out, once hooked, is always improvised.

Fishing on Loon Lake is a community activity. I am joined first and foremost by the loons who swim, dive, and semi-submerge by compressing air out of their feathers. They are superb swimmers, normally using their webbed feet for propulsion and their wings for emergency acceleration. Loons have been found in fishing nets at depths exceeding 250 feet (76 m); they have been caught by accident on live and artificial baits; they have suffered large-scale poisoning after ingesting lead sinkers. But tonight, humanity and loons are at peace as we simply fish a quiet lake together.

Three herring gulls watch intently from a shoal, hoping I'll toss them an unwanted sunfish or bluegill. A chattering kingfisher swoops up into a dead pine on the point, then dive-plops into the lake for a minnow. Overhead, with slow wing flaps, occasional herons "grock" their way home from evening fishing grounds. Now one flushes out of a bay ahead. Countless bullfrogs, snakes, and turtles also prowl the shallows for a fish dinner. A mink trots along a shoreline log, and I pass by an "otter roll" on a natural landing where these fishing members of the weasel family have defecated and generally lolled about. Later, in the dark, raccoons will also hunt the shore, in between snarling fights that echo up and down the lake.

With a startling "thunk" followed by a thundering splash, a big bass hits my surface lure. I set the hook, my reel drag whines when the fish makes a frightened run, and the taut monofilament line throbs and twangs as the bass struggles in the weeds. It *is* a large fish. Too large, I realize, when I see it in my landing net. This female can do more good left to produce more bass in my lake than she can cooking in my frying pan for breakfast tomorrow. I lift her out of the net by the lower lip (which subdues any freshwater bass), carefully remove the hooks, and gently slip her back into her warm rich home.

A tinge of guilt from that muskie? Perhaps. Or maybe after catching so many fish over a lifetime, it just becomes easier to let the big ones go. Now there's the deeper satisfaction of knowing I am helping to ensure that there will be another fish to catch on another day.

Hummingbirds and Cardinal Flowers

IT LOOKS SIMPLE ENOUGH. *The male ruby-throated hummingbird zooms up to a cluster of streambank cardinal flowers, hovers, sips nectar, then zooms away.*

What took three seconds represents the intersection of events that have co-evolved over millennia, so that this hummingbird and the lovely wild lobelia were literally "meant" to meet. It was, and was not, a chance occurrence. On the one hand, there was no certainty that it would happen. On the other hand, Nature had heavily stacked the odds in its favor. Hundreds of millions of similar events animate the Loon Lake ecosystem every day, and their replication everywhere ensures that our larger global life support system can function. Creationists worry that the theory of evolution takes the miracle out of Life, yet a hundred million evolutionary miracles every day account for the aggregated and wonderful miracle of Life itself.

If the pink lady's slipper symbolizes late spring at Loon Lake, then the cardinal flower is the essence of late summer. Its name is no doubt derived from the red robes worn by Roman Catholic cardinals, but I'd rather believe that the human cardinals took their cue from both the bird and the wildflower. In any case, the depth and beauty of that crimson is beyond human description and therefore no doubt divinely inspired.

This plant likes its feet wet. I've found it along the banks of slow streams and the shorelines of lake bays where the wind or freshwater tide keeps the water moving. The cardinal flower holds us in suspense, hesitating till mid- to late summer to bloom, but it is well worth the wait. It stands waist high, with dark green six-inch (15-cm) alternate leaves that are long, narrow, and neatly toothed. But how to describe those flowers? An elongated cluster on an erect stalk? United stamens forming a tube around the style and extending beyond the corolla? I don't think so.

Instead, imagine yourself driving in August along a gravel country road, past a meandering stream surrounded by a lowland thicket of sedges, alder, willow, and winterberry. The dimmer the light, the better. Out of the corner of your eye, you catch a brilliant tiny flash of red buried in its verdant surroundings. A flash only, but undeniably there, about a yard up and close to the water. Hit the brakes. Walk into the wet to join it. Now, behold a loose explosion of dark crimson beauty that could be captured only by a palette knife.

Still, practically speaking, those tubular flowers that most insects find difficult to navigate *do* present a problem for pollination. ... Enter the hummingbird.

I was five when I first noticed hummingbirds visiting the tall purple hollyhocks my mother had planted along the white plastered walls of our small two-story house. I remember marveling at how they could stop in midair and even dart backwards, moving so quickly they seemed to vanish into thin air, then reappear by another bloom. These energetic dynamos buzz back to Canada in May, having wintered somewhere in southern Mexico, or beyond in Central America. (Local lore around Loon Lake has it that they return on the backs of the geese!) In fact, by the time I see it in spring, my hummingbird has crossed the five-hundred-mile (800-km) Gulf of Mexico nonstop, fueled by about two grams of fat. In order to keep its wings in a perpetual blur, one-third of its body is made up of chest muscles. Migrating nonstop over such prodigious distances is especially remarkable when you consider that hummingbirds normally completely refuel every seven to twelve minutes.

Male hummingbirds are in it mainly for the sex. Breeding takes three to five seconds and then they're gone, often as early as July, leaving the female to raise the family on her own. Her nest would be at home in the miniature world of Queen Mab—a tiny cup of bud scales, thistledown, and spider silk. Her eggs are the size of small beans, and her freshly hatched chicks look like blind, naked bees. Once fledged, the young birds are also left to their own devices within a matter of days by their mother, who may head back south as early as late August.

Hummingbirds are entertaining but not gentle creatures. They aggressively defend their territory, and use their acrobatic aerial speed and high-pitched squeaking battle cry to harass and chase off much larger birds. Watching a hummingbird feeder in summer is more like presiding over a war zone.

The hummingbird's delicate needlelike bill opens to reveal a brushy tongue; both features are nicely designed to get at nectar in flowers that is inaccessible to other pollinators. Hummers particularly need nectar in late summer, when the season's young birds are developing their skills at locating food and when extra fuel needs to be taken on board for their impending trek south. They are especially attracted to red. ... Enter the cardinal flower.

Now the evolutionary stage is set. Bird is built and yearning for flower; flower is built and yearning for bird. *The male ruby-throated hummingbird zooms up to a cluster of streambank cardinal flowers, hovers, sips nectar, then zooms away.* As he probes his bill deeper to reach nectar from the bottom of his long flower cup, pollen is deposited on his head in readiness for transfer to another bloom. The metallic red of his throat winks a passing thank-you to his crimson

host, who in return nods its own appreciation in the backwash
of departing wings.

Summer Deer in Jewelweed

IN THE ABSENCE OF snow, anyone alert to bush sign
will instinctively cast an inquiring glance to sand, soft spots,
or muddy areas as a litmus test of what's out and about,
especially in summer. My grandfather, for example, used to
show me deer tracks in the black cultivated soil on the edges
of woodlots lining his fields in northern Saskatchewan.
These shy animals would peek out in the fading light of
evening when my back was turned, as I thinned turnips with
a hoe along planted rows that seemed to disappear on the
horizon.

At Loon Lake, such diagnostic areas for tracks are
coincidentally the natural habitat of jewelweed, or "touch-
me-nots"—beautiful orange-flowered, waist-high plants
whose nickname is derived from a springy elastic seedpod
that bursts open when brushed by a passerby. How such an
ingenious method of dispersing seed evolved is a question
that can be addressed only by what Aristotle called "wonder."
Jewelweed is truly a wonderful wildflower.

And what better "passerby" to catapult jewelweed into
the next generation than one of the largest mammals resident
around Loon Lake, namely, white-tailed deer? And why not
make jewelweed particularly palatable to deer just to
encourage such an encounter?

Now I stare at jewelweed adorning the black mud around a beaver dam that drains down into Loon Lake. Deer tracks dot the mud. The plants have been nipped and fed upon, obviously by deer. Some have been "sprung."

Nature is ingenious; Nature works.

Night Freights

FOR OVER ONE HUNDRED YEARS, the Canadian Pacific Railway main line has passed within earshot of Loon Lake. As sensitive and resistant as wilderness advocates may be to the intruding sounds of civilization, an exception can sometimes be made for the railway. Why is this?

First, many of us have loaded canoes into boxcars and used the railway as a dropoff and pickup point for wilderness trips. This does not mean stopping off at a town, or even a main crossing, but inevitably at such railside markers as "Mile 251," where a particular river or lake intersects the tracks.

Second, the northern railway is cherished as a source of supplies in good times and a secure escape route in bad. For example, on two specific occasions I have had to evacuate seriously injured or sick party members from remote locations in northern Ontario. I remember building a signal fire of creosote ties by the tracks after midnight, and tapping the telegraph wire with a handheld telephone to alert the dispatcher up the line that we needed help. In one case, this involved flagging down the "Canadian," which used to carry

passengers from coast to coast! On another occasion, we
hopped up on one of the inactive engines or "dead units" of
a long freight in the black of night. I thought we were alone,
but after an hour someone struck a match to light a cigarette
and revealed the ghostly faces of three other companions
"riding the rails" at Her Majesty's expense through Chapleau
to Sudbury. I remember that one was a former brakeman,
who talked about being badly beaten up by the "bulls"—
security police employed by the railway. We arrived at
Chapleau at 4:00 a.m., in a heavy rain, at an infirmary staffed
only by a night nurse. She kindly administered a tetanus
shot to our injured companion as a stopgap measure, then
provided us with never-to-be-forgotten dry beds and clean
sheets until a doctor arrived to perform minor surgery in
the morning. We flew back to our base camp in a bush
plane, and since I was sitting in the front next to the pilot,
he decided to turn to me in mid-trip to ask, "Do *you* know
where we are?"

Third, the railway has always been an "as the crow flies"
destination for parties lost in the bush or stranded because
of a canoe broken in rapids. Standard advice in the North is,
"If all else fails, take a bearing, and keep walking till you
hit the railway." For example, in the case of my lost bush
pilot, we agreed to swing north until we could see the railway
and reorient ourselves.

Fourth, the railway has been around long enough in many
parts of this country to become somewhat affectionately
accepted as part of its history. In the case of Loon Lake,
there was the old "K & P" (Kingston to Pembroke) line,
or "Kick & Push" as it became known. Many stops along

the way are still accessible only by rail, which makes them remote in comparison to those on all-season roads.

To be sure, railways are a source of noise and people-caused forest fires. They also kill alarming numbers of wolves, bears, moose, and deer in our national parks. Archie Walker used to lose livestock to trains when railway employees forgot to close gates, though I got the impression that Archie's livestock was often worth more dead and compensated for by the CPR than it was auctioned live at the sales barn. One year a southbound freight hit three of Archie's cows, and a northbound hit his little pigs feeding on what was left of them. It was a sad mess to be sure, especially if you were one of the unfortunate cows or pigs. As it turned out on this occasion, the wandering cows were ruled to be Archie's responsibility, and the fact that the pigs could get at them was the fault of the railway.

Finally, you *can* get used to the sound of trains, even to the point of missing them when they're not around. Not far away, Mike Sagriff worked a lifetime for the railway, then retired in a neat-as-a-pin house fifty-five yards (50 m) from the main line at Wilkinson station, where they used to pump water from Fish Lake into steam locomotives. Somehow, I doubt the night freights disturbed old Mike's sleep. And when, as a boy, I stayed with my grandparents in Nokomos, Saskatchewan, the nearby trains moving grain by night and day had a positively lulling effect on me once I got used to them.

Now at Loon Lake I hear a night freight whistle the standard "two longs—short—long" required for any crossing. I guess that is one signal that has yet to be computerized, because each engineer has a unique signature.

Depending on wind direction and air pressure, it sometimes sounds as if the train is on my doorstep, sometimes far in the distance. In either case, the whippoorwills call throughout its passing and I manage to get a good night's sleep. Consider also that the caboose and conductor have both become extinct in my lifetime, not unlike creatures threatened in the natural world. And in the West, some last remnants of the original tallgrass prairie are to be found only along old railway right-of-ways because they were spared the plow.

So the railway may well be a "mixed blessing," but even that expression acknowledges that it does have something going for it.

Early-Morning Paddle

VERY FEW PEOPLE know how to solo or "single" a canoe properly, by paddling on one side only with the craft well heeled over for direct contact with the water. Your back should rest against the bow thwart so that the canoe actually slips along "backwards," or stern first.

I prefer what is known as the C stroke because it is quieter, more relaxing, and more sustainable than the J stroke, which always struck me as more suited to racing. Both involve a forward stroke followed by a "pry" on a backstroke to keep your craft moving straight ahead. The J is more powerful, executed with a fairly sudden turn or twist of the paddle blade as a pry at the end of the forestroke, leaving a boil of white water behind, whereas the C brings the paddle blade back more smoothly through the water after the

forestroke to pry the canoe gently back onto a straight line.
By modifying the C stroke, it is possible to make stroke after
stroke without ever taking your paddle out of the water.
This permits completely silent travel, without even the sound
of water dripping from your paddle on the recovery or
backswing. "Handy for hunting moose," an Ojibway
schoolmate once remarked.

There are, of course, all kinds of accompanying
maneuvers and fancy strokes, such as braking, drawing,
feathering, figure eights, inside and outside circles, and—
most spectacular of all—the "bow rudder," where the
canoeist leans forward and inserts the paddle blade under
the canoe, causing it to turn on a dime. Some of this stuff is
actually useful, but most of it is adornment bordering on
showing off. The important and fundamental step is for the
single paddler to first learn how to propel the boat cleanly
and effortlessly forward.

I believe this is a skill that must be taught—one of those
things you can best learn by being shown, followed by
practice. But once you've got it, it is yours for life, along
with many peaceful hours of water travel. I learned to canoe
as a young boy and have spent thousands of hours paddling
since, so it has become second nature to me. I am so grateful
to those who taught me, that one of my greatest pleasures is
to return the favor by helping anyone who conveniently asks,
"Hey, how do you *do* that anyway?"

Now it's a late August morning, barely light. A rolling
mist on Loon Lake lures me from coffee on the cabin
screened porch. My canoe is dew-drenched and feels wet
against my thighs as I gently lever and slip the stern into the

lake. For a kneepad, I have one of Evan's cherished old plaid shirts, so in a symbolic way he can still enjoy the ride with me. My paddle is black cherry, light but strong, with a traditional beaver-tail-shaped blade and a handcrafted butt that fits comfortably across my palm. A good paddle feels totally familiar and eager to work. With a shove I'm launched, settled, and buoyant ... stroke, stroke.

The lake feels warm against my fingertips occasionally dipping into the water where the paddle shaft flares into the blade. This warmth is the stored energy of long days under a steady summer sun, now felt in contrast to cooler morning air. The mist is also caused by the difference between air and water temperatures. It appeared to be everywhere from a distance, but it is seemingly nowhere now that I'm actually in it. It's as if I can't see where I'm going, but I always know where I am. I once used only a map and compass to blindly cross a large lake by canoe in morning fog, and found it an uncomfortable and eerie act of faith to find my way with nothing land-fast to use as a bearing. Just trust what guides you, and you will get to where you are meant to go ... stroke, stroke.

Now, as the morning mist burns off Loon Lake, the pool of visibility surrounding my canoe gradually becomes larger. I paddle the shoreline, whose every stump and fern is set above a great shimmering mirror. Swarming out into the lake from the land are troops of pickerelweed with heart-shaped leaves jutting in different directions above the water to reveal occasional lavender flowers. Further out are flotillas of yellow bullheads and white water lilies still closed in big morning buds among floating pads. A few soft maples in the low spots are already turning red, and a heavy cone crop glows yellow-green in the crowns of mature white pines—another of summer's solar legacies ... stroke, stroke.

The loons, with no chicks this year, flapped off the lake at dawn to visit neighbors nearby. Sure enough, I can now hear loons flying high and calling to others on the water below in the distance. A heron croaks once overhead on its way to somewhere else. Flycatchers flit out and back from their perches to catch breakfast. A catbird mews from somewhere deep inside a winterberry bush. Blue jays that were quiet earlier in the summer, while raising their young, are now back to their noisy selves. And a flock of crows raucously dive-bombs a great horned owl now that daylight gives them the courage to do so ... stroke, stroke.

Backlit spiderwebs traced in dew hang expectantly from low snags. Waterstriders randomly scurry patterns on the lake's surface. Crickets chirp steadily from the wet ground. And the sun is now high enough for cicadas to tentatively start up their rhythmic summer whine from the trees ... stroke, stroke.

Surprisingly far out in the lake, I encounter a huge snapping turtle, bobbing head-down and treading water with its massive front claws, so that only the rear of its shell and spiny tail stick up out of the water. It appears to be busy scanning below, unaware that I'm approaching until I'm right beside it, at which point the turtle matter-of-factly shifts from neutral to forward and pulls its way downward, out of sight. Its tail descends like some prehistoric periscope. Few creatures look as fierce head-on as a snapping turtle. I remember brushing my teeth one evening at lakeside when a large snapping turtle loomed straight up toward me just as I stooped to rinse. With our faces only inches apart, I'm not sure who looked more frightening to whom, but we both retreated with a start and, in my case, crestfallen ... stroke, stroke.

Now the sun has almost completely burned off the mist, the cicadas are in full song, and the first of the day's breezes is afoot to stir both lake and leaves. I'm ready for breakfast.

Summer Storm

H O T , H U M I D summer days at Loon Lake adhere to a pattern. Dawn breaks clear, or with wispy high cirrus clouds that gradually give way to cumulus puffs in the northwest by midday. Then, around afternoon tea, someone in the heavens decides whether a spectacular sunset will be enough on its own, or whether Earth will be blessed with a spectacular thunderstorm thrown in for good measure.

This afternoon is definitely headed toward thunderstorm. Gradually, giant cumulonimbus clouds with anvil tops are towering, building, and billowing. If I concentrate my gaze on their outer margins I can actually see these turbulent rainclouds ominously growing. At my end of the lake, the sun and blue sky reign as usual, but, out beyond the far end, trouble is brewing. Slowly, inevitably, the thunderheads fill first a third, then two-thirds, then all of my field of view.

The lake goes from friendly slapping wavelets to a dark flat calm. Then a disturbingly cool breeze comes straight at me. Thunder rumbles, seemingly far away. But, as the thunderheads turn indigo overhead with a frightening tinge of yellow, the wind picks up.

I can hear it coming through the trees. ...

Now squalls race randomly down the lake until a steady tide of whitecaps takes over. Sheet lightning jumps from cloud to cloud in the distance, then becomes ground lightning, moving closer and closer until bolts hit trees all around me in simultaneous "Bangs!" and flashes. This is no time to be out on the water.

Fat, heavy raindrops slant, slash, and disintegrate through my cabin's screened porch. They are quickly transformed into a curtain of windblown rain that pounds on my cabin roof so loudly a person would have to shout to be heard. I retreat from the porch into the cabin. For five minutes, violent rain-filled gusts beat down on Loon Lake, then cold hail bounces off the rocks and peppers the forest.

It all lets up as quickly as it came. The hail lasts only a minute or so, leaving tiny short-lived ice balls melting into granite crannies and bringing with it a cooling fog. Light misty rain continues, until the sun reappears to calm everything with a silent moist rainbow. New fresh puddles are scattered everywhere, and slick wet leaves drip, drip, drip.

The summer storm sweeps on into the southeast, crackling and rumbling its way into a distant land. Loon Lake, however, has already settled down. Some clouds remain, but eventually break up, allowing shafts of evening sunlight to stream through a soft mist rising from quick-cooled earth. Now everything is aftermath. Drenched. Refreshed. Ready to grow some more.

Evening Song

BY LATE AFTERNOON, busy gray catbirds are mewing
in my blueberry bushes while yanking fruit from the lower
branches. By suppertime, veeries in thick cover send
crescendos of flutelike variations out over the lake, robins
cluck and jostle in the winterberry, and a white-throated
sparrow pipes up clearly from the shoreline alders. As the
light dims, an evening flight of wood ducks whistles overhead
and a heron quietly flaps out of its favorite fishing spot.
Its silhouette shows the heron's neck folded comfortably
so that its own back becomes a headrest. By dusk, over the
ambient drone of mosquitoes, nighthawks high above
"peeet!" their way randomly across the sky, mouths agape to
swallow insects on the wing. By dark, a whippoorwill chants
rhythmically to anyone who will listen, again, again, and
again. And by midnight, the loons join the bullfrogs for a
moonlight serenade.

Growth

SUMMER IS A SEASON of growth. This is when terminal
shoots on white pines spurt, as do the legs of lanky adolescent
coyotes. Game trails become green and overgrown; beaver
ponds thicken with new life and color—blue flag, pink
pogonias, yellow bladderworts, and white water lilies. Spring
leaves become food for waves of summer munchers, and a

second generation of "summer leaves" appears, yearning
for the Sun's vital heat. Ferns unfurl, enlarge, and yellow;
birds hatch, fledge, and fly; fish spawn, nest, and retreat. In
summer, the living is easy enough here in the North that bits
of life which arrived from the South in spring concentrate,
reproduce, and thrive in this part of the world.

Yet, by midsummer, the shorebirds are already reversing
the flow. And by August their migration is fully under way.
That pair of spotted sandpipers bobbing restlessly along a
northern gravel bar is bidding the season of growth farewell.
Many more will follow.

Summer is a time much recollected—a crucible of
warmth and activity. It provides a prolonged pulse of fresh
blood that fuels Nature for the rest of the year.

Fall

S E P T E M B E R – N O V E M B E R

Harbingers

PERHAPS IT IS BECAUSE they grow so weary of winter that northern people look so eagerly for early signs of spring. But for me, since fall is my favorite season, I particularly crave its advance notices.

Look for the brilliant summer yellow on male goldfinches beginning to diminish and show hints of winter olive; for parched ferns and the first flaming leaves of soft maples in damp lowlands; for goldenrod, and blue and white asters, now blooming side by side in old fields; for the first scarlet traces on sumac leaves, and maroon hues in the ashes on upland ridges; for wild grape turning purple, and Virginia creeper turning dark red along fence lines; for tan grasses heavy with seed; for blackbirds beginning to flock; and for early flights of ducks at dawn or dusk now that the adults have finished the molt. Look also for pitchers of fresh cold draft beer in the local tavern to slake throats, made thirsty by swathing and baling the second cut of hay in dusty late-summer heat.

Fall is in the air. Now I can walk through heavy cover back to my furthest beaver ponds completely unmolested by mosquitoes and deerflies. Sleep at night is deeper, because the air temperature is consistently cooler. The tops of familiar winter constellations show themselves in the East before dawn. Afternoons are less humid, as thunderheads have ceded to fairer skies, and news arrives of the first hurricanes along the U.S. southeastern seaboard. The last of the sweet corn is being picked, pickles and relishes are set down, squash is coming on, farm bins are full, and rural towns take turns staging fall fairs.

Autumn is also the time of year when I find it achingly difficult to work at a desk in the city. For thirty years now, I have been reliably out of the office and "unreachable" during early October. And forget trying to arrange meetings during hunting season in the North. For that matter, forget trying to keep kids in school or men and women on the job. They have better things to do. They will not forgo this traditional time in camps out on the land. That honey-colored harvest moon hovering over fresh-cut barley is also the hunter's moon hovering over a wall-tent glowing mellow from the kerosene lamp within.

Fall gets in the blood; it will not be denied.

Land Ethics and the Kitchen Table

IN CONSERVATION, as in many other human endeavors, we must never confuse process with progress, or progress with success. Great ideas, plans, and statements of good intentions are all very fine, as are any number of bureaucratic "implementation mechanisms." But in the end, what matters is what actually happens on the ground. I cite for authority Winston Churchill, who observed, "When all is said and done, more is said than done"; Aldo Leopold, who urged us to measure conservation progress "on the back forty"; and a good friend who raises cattle for a living, "All this gum flap ain't worth a cow flap."

In order to make a difference on the ground, in order to take root and really last, conservation proposals must be embraced, promoted, and championed (not just "accepted") by those who depend on the affected lands and waters. The fact that so many of the conservation movement's ideas are seen as being insensitive to local interests, or pushed through despite them, has left a legacy of bitterness and an understandable image of conservation advocates being urban thinkers out of touch with rural reality. Therefore, I find it helpful to put what might seem like a good idea "in the office" to this simple test: "Would it sell over the kitchen table?"

In other words, take this idea, hop in a pickup, drive up the farm lane, and if you are fortunate enough to be invited to sit down for a chat about it over coffee in the kitchen, does it fly? (Hint: Remember that the person you are talking to likely knows more about the area of interest than you do, and that the area probably wouldn't even *be* of interest to you if he or she had not done a pretty good job of looking after it so far.)

For me, owning 270 acres (110 ha) of bush on Loon Lake has put me on the receiving end of many "good ideas," which I have actively and professionally promoted elsewhere. Now, however, it is my turn to negotiate and implement a land ethic in practical terms over my own kitchen table. This is because land ownership brings with it the legal and moral right to determine what happens to the land I own. This right, which entails an obligation, is inescapable. It is exercised, either by design or by default, by proactively deciding what I want for my land and by permitting or not permitting various uses proposed by others who drive up *my* lane.

To proactively decide what I want for my land, I have developed a Conservation Agreement that outlines specific restrictions——things I *don't* want to have happen. These include commercial logging and mining, human alteration of the watershed, hydro power run into my cabin, mechanized travel anywhere but on the drive in, and exterior lighting that obliterates a naturally dark night sky. Such restrictions are now registered on title, and for 999 years will be legally binding on all future owners of the property. Whether this agreement saddles them with wisdom or simply with my personal prejudices will be borne out over the next ten centuries. I don't particularly care, because like it or not, the land will be protected. But preparing such an agreement certainly has involved thinking through why this place is important to me, what I value about it, and therefore what uses I consider compatible or not compatible with those values.

Responding to those who come down my lane, on the other hand, has given me a chance to understand what value *others* see in my land. It puts me in the position of having to say yes or no to their requests, and it requires that I explain in plain language why I agree or disagree. Being indecisive is not really an option in these circumstances.

For example, here comes one of the local hunt clubs. With permission from the landowner, this particular club has hunted deer for more than thirty years on this land, beginning before I owned it, and every year they check in to see if it's all right again. "Yes" is my answer, "but you know the conditions: no littering as you travel through the bush or around the campfires at your watches. No flagging or blazing of trails. No travel by motorized means, so you have to know the country well enough to walk in and out in the dark. If you're successful, carry your deer out the hard way. No shooting at anything else, like bears and coyotes, because I like having them around. And if you guys can find out who has been ripping out the beaver dam in my back pond, I'd be much obliged."

In exchange for hunting privileges, the hunt club provides me with modest payment, which makes a contribution to the taxes. They also run off anyone else they find hunting on my place in November, leaving me with a pretty good idea of who is and isn't on the property at this time of year. These arrangements have evolved and worked over the years for successive generations of hunters and land owners alike. We both gain: we both drop in on each other periodically; we stop and chat when we meet on the road; we trade notes on where the hunting and fishing are good this year, on land sales, house fires, construction, poaching charges, family feuds, taxes, and what the municipal council has been up to lately.

Now, here come members of the Kingston Field Naturalists, who monitor my Conservation Agreement on behalf of the Nature Conservancy of Canada. Can they come in and hike around to "update their inventory of the flora and fauna," which, translated, means have fun finding birds, plants, reptiles, amphibians, and just about anything else of natural interest? "Yes, please, because I always learn something new from you folks. I'll make arrangements with my nearest neighbor, Francis Walker, to let you in if I'm not here. But let me know when you're coming, won't you? I'd love to join you."

Here's the trapper from Echo Lake. Can he trap on my place, or at least travel over it to access his trapline on Crown land to the northwest? "Sorry, no. I'm still not convinced that drowning sets for beaver and muskrat are very humane. I enjoy watching the otters. And the fisher keep the porcupines in check. Even though I know you wouldn't trap the beaver completely out, I have no real way of controlling how many you take, and I need them to maintain my ponds for the Blanding's turtles. Still, I'm interested in hearing how you do up there, so let's keep in touch. How many fisher did you say you caught last year?" Then, in the course of chatting some more, we discover that those are my tracks he sees, and his I see, because we're about the only two people in the county who get way up into the backcountry in winter.

Now, here comes a volunteer fireman from town inquiring whether I would like to sell my land, because he's looking for a place to hunt. "No thanks, but if I change my mind I'll let you know." All right, but how about letting him cut some standing dead timber in that swamp by the bend in the road where it could be easily skidded out? "Sorry again, I've got wood ducks and swallows nesting in those snags, and I like to leave as many as possible for them. By the way, just how long would it take you guys to get up here if my cabin ever caught fire?"

Now, here is a local resident who ran for council. Can she come in when I'm not here to fish with her nephew? She has lived in the area all her life and used to fish in Loon Lake "all the time" with her brother. "Hmmm ... okay, but no power boats, because I don't want gas and oil in the lake. You're welcome to use my rowboat though. And only if you are with Francis Walker, who has to let you in anyway." (This way, I avoid my permission being handed on by her to any number of other friends and relatives coming in unaccompanied, which would quickly lead to such a small lake being fished out.) "What do you think of the new reeve?"

Now, here's Francis himself, dropping in for a game of cribbage. "Come on in, my friend! How's your mother doing since I last saw her?"

And so it goes, the ongoing juggling of local interests in an attempt to be fair. When there is work to be done, like when Evan wanted a fence strung "horse high and hog tight" to demarcate his land flooded and expropriated by the Conservation Authority, the contract went to Archie Walker because he knew how to build a good fence over rough country. Archie also helped collect money for Christmas trees sold to local residents off Evan's land, ten dollars a tree—half of which went to Archie. And he delivered the occasional load of wood, because Evan would rather spend time planting or pruning live trees than sawing up dead ones.

Now Archie's son, Francis, and I are continuing the tradition and doing business together. For example, he built a cedar-log-and-stone crib to anchor my gate, shared a load of gravel with me to fill some holes in the drive in, and helped his brother-in-law put new shingles on my cabin roof. Since he is handy with a saw and has a portable wood splitter driven by the hydraulics off his tractor, Francis has helped me remove a few big dead black oaks that might have fallen on my cabin or drive in, then split them into many winters' worth of firewood in a fraction of the time it would take me to do the job by hand.

These are the kinds of personal relationships and on-the-spot judgment calls that translate otherwise abstract ideas into something that hits the ground, and is meaningful to practical people and the land itself. I'm sure I get a lot of it wrong. Still, I have to say yes or no to the various requests made of me. I have to do my best by my land *and* by my neighbors. Besides, it's fun. And I always learn something. It starts with shutting up and listening. It means having the "gift of the gab" and jawing over the fender of a pickup. It involves extending simple human decency and respect, and taking a genuine interest in other people's lives, for example, by helping Francis when he needed a generator in the ice storm of '98, by providing paid work at fair wages to local residents, by helping an elderly farmer out of his tractor cab when it capsized in the ditch, by paying my last respects at the funeral home when Archie died, and by quietly visiting his grave in the small cemetery overlooking the rocky land that so grudgingly provided a living for Archie and his large family.

We conservationists are fond of despairing until the rest of the world comes around to our way of thinking. But maybe we would be more successful by occasionally putting ourselves in the rest of the world's shoes, recognizing that not everyone sees the world the way we do. It is fascinating to me that people with strongly held positions find it so difficult to acknowledge merit in the points made by the other side. Many advocates confuse being fair with being weak, whereas the strongest advocates are those perceived to be the fairest. After all, it's usually easy to make sense to each other. But how do we do over the kitchen table?

October

N O T H I N G   C O U L D   B E   more liberating for the human spirit than a backpack with a few light supplies and enough free days in October to follow my nose or a compass bearing anywhere I wish. My father taught me (and eight other boys) how to use a map and compass; we were all striving to earn our "Pathfinder's Badge" for the Whitedog Falls Scout Troop No. 1 (there was no No. 2). By the time we were through, each of us could accurately pace off distances over land, estimate long ones over water, and arrive reliably at target destinations deep in never-before-visited bush, through the magic of orienteering. Some of my happiest (and proudest) days were spent on those hikes with my father, especially in October.

Now at this time of the year, for which all other months are just a "fitting interlude," my cabin on Loon Lake becomes more of a staging point or a base camp than any kind of permanent home. Usually each day's travel ends with a glimpse of what Sig Olson at the end of a portage called "that glorious blue through the trees"—in my case a small remote lake on whose shores I will camp for the night. Therefore I can visit as many lakes as I have days available to ramble.

Lunch is prepared in the morning and eaten on the move on any sunny spot with a view. Dinner is cooked over an open fire, and might be a partridge flushed during the day, or a fresh bass taken casting from the shoreline in early evening. Sometimes I pack a tent; sometimes I build a rough shelter; sometimes I just sleep out under the stars.

Times like this have a way of making important meetings with ministers, CEOs, and grand chiefs seem less important, along with urgent memos, priority tasks, keynote speeches, and crucial decisions. The always-blinking "message waiting" light on hotel telephones seems far away, and I have no need of an airline boarding pass to start tomorrow's journey. For now, all that matters is finding a dry spot in the deep, soft moss where I can get a comfortable night's sleep.

The irony is that we commit so much of life to things that are unimportant, or which we come to regret; the tragedy is that we do so knowingly. I cannot imagine ever regretting these bonding moments with the land in October, but I may well wish there had been more of them.

Autumn's Glow

A FRIEND FROM ENGLAND once remarked that he had no idea so much brilliant color could occur in Nature as in the Canadian hardwood forests of autumn. He was a renowned gourmet caterer, and the only person I know to have packed a lettuce spinner from Loon into Basshook Lake. Another friend, having moved to B.C. after living fifty years in Ontario, frequently remarks how he misses the fall color of the East. He is a renowned Canadian wildlife artist, who I think might agree that we can come closer to capturing that color in paint rather than words, but still only close. In the caterer's case, any description of autumn's glow would have been inadequate because he had not actually seen it; in the artist's case, it would be inadequate because he has.

A third friend came as close as anyone to capturing what I am talking about, and I had the privilege of painting with him one day on Georgian Bay. That was A.Y. Jackson, the renowned member of the Group of Seven. My lasting memory of "A.Y." is not so much our painting together, as it was watching his stout, elderly form glide quietly off the rocks into rising mists for an early-morning swim. How often, I wondered, had this great man enjoyed the solitude of similar moments in Algoma country, Quebec, or Algonquin Park? His strong northern spirit has been an inspiration to us all, and that spirit was never stronger than when it was out on the land in the fall.

So for me, fall color simply eludes description. It is, instead, a feeling. The raw yellows, oranges, reds, burgundies, and browns of poplars, hard and soft maples, ashes, and oaks are breathtaking individually, but deeply evocative together. Each leaf and tree appears against an autumnal backdrop, yet each in turn contributes to that backdrop. The combined effect is a seasonal glow that increases steadily through September, reaches maximum intensity in early October, then wanes by November.

This October day began for my daughter, Robin, and me at 5:30 a.m. Together we walked for half an hour through

the woods in the dark to stand by a silent beaver pond while
the stars still reflected on its surface. A moonlit muskrat
quietly plied a rippled path to a loafing log, where it sat up
to chew on marsh sedges. Robin counted four meteors in the
first two minutes. Shortly after six o'clock, as the East began
to lighten, the moon and stars gradually loosened their hold
on the night. At six-thirty, still well before sunrise, we first
saw the glow—just a hint of orange, radiating even in the
semi-dark from a pondside sugar maple across the water
and down to our left. With each succeeding minute, others
joined in—first the yellow-oranges, then the orange-reds,
then the red-browns. Irrepressibly, the glow grew warmer
like a fanned ember, bursting into flame when a low October
morning sun caught just the tops of the trees like waiting
torches. As we walked back to the cabin for breakfast, the
tree torches steadily burned further down their trunks, until
sunlight flooded in all around us, backlighting the canopy
above, brightening the rock-moss ridges ahead, and pooling
here and there on the forest floor. Now, we were fully *in* the
glow, warmly enveloped by autumn itself.

Later this day, we walked wherever we wished, on light
trails of our own making and on those of the deer. We rested
in shady, cool grottoes by ponds. We enjoyed the fall breeze
on our faces from sunny lookouts. I noticed how beautiful
things in Nature appear against other things in the fall.
White birch trunks contrast with a shimmering leafy yellow
background. Dark green pines of all sizes stand out among
the brightly colored hardwoods. Fall's palette blends in a
pond's reflection, or a single bright red maple leaf comes
crisply into focus against the pond-water's melded curtain.

Autumn gold is set against the bright blue of a clear, cool sky or a choppy wild lake. Orange hues stand out against white wispy clouds or the grays of gathering rains. And brilliant red winterberries are cast against the muted misty purples of a marsh or distant hills.

As the day progressed, the glow shifted in mood. From the pre-glow before sunrise and the low light of morning, it grew in intensity to the full overhead brilliance of midday so often depicted on postcards and calendars. Then it softened gradually through the lowering light and lengthening shadows of late afternoon to embrace sunset with a brief evening afterglow. Next, the stars resumed their watch and the glow took its rest. Even in the dark, however, a flashlight or vehicle headlights will reveal it still alive, waiting, and ready to glow again tomorrow.

Only the hard frosts of late October and the rain-laden winds of November can dim autumn's glow for another year. It is snuffed out finally by the first heavy snow, but continues to rattle defiance in the form of parchment-colored beech leaves stubbornly clinging to smooth gray limbs through winter.

For me, fall at Loon Lake is tinged with sadness. Yet it is the kind of sadness I yearn to feel. I seek to be alone. I find myself stopping more frequently along the trail, and lingering longer. I remember things from the past and reflect on their meaning. I feel an upwelling of emotion, and tears are always close to the surface. Perhaps it is because this season is so unimaginably beautiful and so deeply personal. Or perhaps it is because fall is when the land speaks straight to our hearts.

Thinking Like a Warbler

DEPENDING UPON your temperament, identifying fall wood warblers is either a birder's worst nightmare or an exquisite challenge. This is because birds in this family degenerate from their fiery spring uniforms with distinctive bright splashes of yellow, orange, chestnut, and blue into autumn fatigues showing only drab olives, creams, and tans.

My personal favorite is the myrtle warbler, which according to a 1973 edict of the American Ornithological Union Checklist Committee has now been assigned the undignified and less lyrical name of "yellow-rumped warbler." (I cannot imagine that any woman named Myrtle would be thrilled.)

I am partial to this warbler because the male retains dabs of yellow on its crown, on either side of its breast and, yes, on its rump throughout the year, which makes it quite easy to identify. The yellow-rumped warbler breeds right across Canada, including a British Columbia population that used to be known as Audubon's warbler, and it is probably the most abundant wood warbler in our country, especially in fall migration. It is also the largest and hardiest of the wood warblers—the first one I see moving through in the spring and the last one I see in the fall—because it is capable of switching from a diet of insects, many of which are not available at these times of the year, to one of berries and seeds. I have seen a myrtle warbler literally light up the somber woods of November at Loon Lake.

Ornithologists fill bookshelves with publications that impersonally aggregate thousands of human experiences and hard-won field observations into range maps of North America that appear in a postage-stamp-sized square, opposite a terse description of identifying features. But now it is late October and my sleeves are rolled up to feel cool autumn on my arms as I cut wood. I stop long enough to squint at something, not inert on the page of a field guide, but there, pert and alive, just ten yards away in a clump of alders. Sure enough, it's a male myrtle warbler, glimpsed for a few seconds by me while I was in the midst of doing something else. Only later that night, when he was long gone and traveling a hundred miles further south, did I bother to think like a warbler and reflect on what lay behind and ahead for my momentary companion.

This cheerful spirit nested in a black spruce in the boreal forest of Quebec, flitting by day all summer among white spruce, balsam fir, jack pine, white birch, and trembling aspen to catch enough insects for himself and his family. Then, by September, a new urge caused him to change his normal daytime activities in preparation for an inverted schedule of extreme exertion by night. Nocturnal migration offers many advantages to songbirds—the chance to forage for food during daytime rest periods, and to experience cooler temperatures, less turbulent air, and fewer predators during nighttime travel.

My friend instinctively built up his fat reserves by gorging on insects and berries till mid-October; then, one day, he lifted off at dusk and climbed quickly to an altitude of 1,600 feet (500 meters). At this point, his tiny brain engaged a miniature compass whose accomplishments rival those of the most advanced navigational circuitry developed by humans. Nature's complex orienting clues for this flying object's flight path include the moon, the stars, the setting and rising sun, the Earth's magnetic field, polarized light in the sky, and topographical features interpreted from a dimly lit landscape below. So, with nothing but God-given guideposts, my southbound myrtle warbler set off to traverse no fewer than three countries, nine provinces and states, and ten major forest regions of North America. ...

From the boreal forest of Quebec he entered the red and white pine, hemlock, yellow birch, maple, and oak of the Great Lakes–St. Lawrence forest spanning Quebec and Ontario. This is where he encountered me, cutting wood by a lowland thicket. Then he pressed on, leaving the Canadian Shield for the sedimentary limestone country of eastern Lake Ontario, which he skirted to enter the northern hardwood stands of upstate New York. Here he staged in birch, beech, maple, and hemlock. Catching the northeast side of the Appalachian Mountains, he flew on into the southern hardwoods of Pennsylvania, where chestnut, oak, hickory, and yellow poplar provided rest and refuge by day. Then, on into the night, to the oak–pine hardwood forests of Virginia and the Carolinas. And still on, into the southeastern pine forests of Georgia and Florida, where he put down into longleaf, loblolly, and slash pine. Here he also flew over what's left of the southeastern bottomlands—fingerlike fragments of cypress, tupelo, and sweet gum that once cloaked these great river valleys draining gently down into the Atlantic Ocean. Then on, ever southward, down the

Florida peninsula, over the drowned Everglades, until he staged and recharged again in remnant subtropical mangrove forests looking out onto the Gulf of Mexico. Here, one last refuel before he followed the Keys, then flew out over the ocean to land in his dry, warm destination—the cactus scrub and the Cuban pines and oaks of the Greater Antilles. At this point, many of his cousins added still one more leg to their journey, out over Jamaica, and then the gleaming Caribbean, to finally rest and reside in the rain-drenched forests of Panama.

The changing natural textures of all these different forest types offered my myrtle warbler both sanctuary and nourishment as he rode the rushing tide of life southward in fall. Storms and fog slowed him down to be sure, but most inclement weather is survivable by hunkering down until it passes. However, this warbler also had a better-than-even chance of encountering urban areas whose tall, lighted structures already block forty-one percent of North America's east–west horizon from his vantage point, even more when we just consider the city-strewn East. Migrating birds are disoriented by tall night-lit buildings, and cannot cope with windows that are not visible to them by day or night. In Toronto alone, we have documented and retrieved over a hundred different species of birds that have collided with buildings (myrtle warblers rank among the top twenty-five most vulnerable species), and it has been estimated that up to 100 million birds die in this fashion every year in North America. Therefore, if more people thought like a warbler, they would turn their lights out during bird migration periods.

The same is true of degrading or destroying the forests upon which warblers depend. Although we in the North have rightly rallied to the cause of slowing down destruction of tropical forests, the fact is that we have lost or degraded a much larger proportion of our own northern temperate stands. And pesticides applied in both North and South are known to concentrate in insect-eating birds that pick up prohibitive loadings of these poisons from their prey. Ironically, these same birds are wonderful natural predators on the very insects we seek to control with such biocides.

Thinking like a warbler would give us pause, because there is wisdom in these most diminutive creatures—wisdom that, if followed, would help us save them ... and ourselves.

Forest Floor

WHEN I WAS A graduate student, in order to determine the species and abundance of plants regenerating under a jack pine forest after fire, I established and inventoried hundreds of one-meter quadrats along transects through fourteen different forest plots. This expression, "one-meter quadrat," is variously loathed or loved by students of botany or forestry, depending on how many they had to monitor. A variation on this sampling technique is to actually fashion a one-meter quadrat from a frame of wood or aluminum, then cast it randomly into the area being studied, to carefully document everything that occurs within that square meter wherever the frame falls. I'm sure that more than one student, after a thousand or so square meters, has pitched this sampling device into the lake. In any case, being on your hands and knees, and pawing through the vegetation with one hand, while making note of it on a clipboard with the other, develops a lifelong appreciation for the complexity and importance of the forest floor.

Now it is November, so leaf-fall is more or less finished at Loon Lake. In a fit of nostalgia, I toss a one-meter square off the trail onto the forest floor in a typical spot (a lowland site with granite outcrops nearby) to count leaves. I discover the following:

Species	*No. of leaves / sq. m*
Winterberry	1,100
Red maple	700
Red oak	525
Alder	425
White oak	325
White birch	275
Serviceberry	250
Sugar maple	150
Sweetfern	50
Dogwood	25
TOTAL	*3,825*

These are the leafy bits and pieces that thrive in and help build "black gold"—soil. Over ninety percent of the biological richness of northern temperate ecosystems is locked up in this "dark laboratory," specifically in the top few inches, or humus layer, which has accumulated over centuries. Humus is built from what foresters call "litter" on the surface, and litter's most important component at Loon Lake is clearly millions of tons of fallen leaves. This treasure of stored biological wealth provides the nutrient base for my forest to regenerate after disturbances such as fire. In fact, fire enriches that base and adds even more wealth to the buried treasure.

This natural dynamic contrasts dramatically with tropical forest ecosystems, where the reverse is true—most of the biological richness is locked up in trunks, branches, and living leaves *above* the forest floor. If these are removed, for example, by slashing and burning, there is much less capacity in the soil to support the nutrient demands of activities such as agriculture and successive harvests of trees, which may last only two or three rotations at best. The natural tropical forest system, resilient and prepared as it may be for Nature's changes, just never evolved to support this kind of human disturbance.

Back at Loon Lake, my single sample of 3,825 leaves on the forest floor represented a *square* meter on the surface only. A *cubic* meter would have revealed millions of soil organisms, without which litter could never become humus. Furthermore, this was only one square meter out of the 1,092,675 square meters that make up my property, let alone the township, the county, the province, the country, the continent, and the world. What emerges is a precious, thin layer of life from which all other living things ultimately derive. This is why systems ecologists refer to concepts such as "the nutrient ceiling" when hypothesizing what the ultimate limiting factors or carrying capacity might be for Earth's different ecosystems.

This also explains why one of the most important (and overlooked) publications in Canadian parliamentary history was *Soil at Risk: Canada's Eroding Future*, the 1984 report of a standing Senate committee chaired by Senator Herb Sparrow. Senator Sparrow valiantly traveled back and forth across the country, first to chair hearings, then to energetically couch the final report's message in popular terms to awaken a complacent public and policy-makers alike. The net effect has been disappointing, but the study still speaks wisely to us all, as our national band of black gold becomes poorer by the day.

In the fall, a one-meter square could be cast anywhere on the forest floor around Loon Lake to frame a biological and artistic masterpiece—new autumn leaves splashed with colors beyond any painterly ambition, and fresh clean fragrances beyond any perfume manufacturer's capability. As October's frost gives way to November's ice, these millions of masterpieces are glazed and preserved under the snow for winter, awaiting rediscovery in their gallery on the ground next April. Until then, a thought cast back will recapture some reminiscent taste of the glory that went before.

Crinkling Ice

IN NOVEMBER, an intense, solemn peace settles on Loon Lake. The occasional call of a wayward jay or crow only momentarily breaks an enveloping silence on the land. This deeper and deeper quiet fills longer and longer intervals between fewer and fewer disturbances, as the inevitable grip of winter gradually takes hold everywhere.

The bays freeze first, during clear starry nights, leaving an ice edge that partially recedes under the next day's sun and waves. This is when hardy divers such as American mergansers, goldeneyes, buffleheads, and scaup pay my lake a late staging visit, bobbing on the last patches of open water against the season's first skiffles of snow. Gradually the nights get colder, and so do the days, allowing the ice to take over shrinking open areas out in the center of the lake, until a thin pane of frozen fresh water glistens across its full length and breadth. Now, no wave laps. No songbird sings. The North is ready.

On such an afternoon, I sit in my cabin screened porch, warmed by a light down-filled jacket and a cup of hot coffee, idly waiting for anything to make a sound, anywhere. But there is nothing. Another sip of coffee. Still nothing. For fully half an hour I hear only my own breathing, the gentle creak of my wooden chair, and the rasp of my jacket sleeve against my front as I raise and lower my cup. I resolve to out wait the silence. . . .

Then, out of sight, deep in the alders, there is the clear sound of thin ice being broken by a single footstep down by the shore. I am reminded of pushing my boots, as a boy, through the smooth new ice full of air bubbles that first covered puddles, sending shards of clear ice tinkling like broken glass out over the rest of the puddle's frozen surface. Whatever made this first step today made so much noise that it stopped immediately, as if in surprise, hesitating in order to decide whether it was wise to go any further.

But now there is another step, either backward (in which case I imagine this is all I am going to hear) or forward (in which case there is going to be more). Silence. It must have been forward, because now a confident racket sets in, as whatever this is has obviously decided to plow ahead. For ten minutes I listen to something unseen steadily breaking ice out from the shore, working its way ahead until it is close to being in clear view. Is it my imagination, or is this thing deliberately making more and more noise as it goes, and *enjoying* it?

The happy, bounding rhythm of the crinkling ice now confirms my hunch that an otter, for some reason, is going for a late-afternoon romp. Sure enough, the otter finally appears out in the open, well beyond the alders, playfully crushing its way toward a single log frozen into the lake's surface about seventy-five yards offshore.

My binoculars reveal, up close, the sheer zest of what is going on. Using the thrust of its tail and webbed hind feet, the otter propels the front of its body up over the new ice, enthusiastically leaping ahead like a crazed Labrador retriever chasing the duck of its dreams. But unlike the dog, the otter intersperses its bounds forward with the odd splashing somersault and slippery figure eight backwards, just to revel in its own wake filled with mini-icepans. The result is a noisy, recklessly splashing display of energy, unlike anything I have ever seen.

And the purpose of the whole exercise? Apparently to haul out on that lonely log, bask in the last of the day's sun for a few minutes, then whimsically slither and ripple its way back to shore along its own broken path through the ice.

In an era when indoor ecologists armed with computer models try to reduce everything they (or others) observe in

Nature to the most efficient investment of energy, the North American river otter stands as a wonderful enigma. So much of what it does appears to have little or no strict "survival value." Or perhaps the otter has been so efficiently designed that it has enough surplus energy to actually *enjoy* surviving? Whether by design or delight, this frisky weasel can make fun of even moody November.

Legacy

THE MOODS OF AUTUMN evoke deep memories of the past and move me to take stock. This is when the spirit of conservation leaders who went before inhabits the land and encourages those of us still alive to mind the store. Their legacy of books, speeches, and conservation accomplishments is now on the record, serving as a body of work to which we can return for inspiration and guidance. Their traces also persist in the bush, if you know where to look: old blackened rocks arranged for a cooking fire; a blaze here and there to locate a portage at night; tent poles cut and left leaning up out of consideration for the next traveler; a crease of red or green paint off an old canvas-covered Chestnut canoe on a hidden boulder in the rapids; perhaps a touch of oil paint or acrylics where a palette knife was quickly scraped clean. Their faces haunt September's clouds. Their passion brightens October's forest. Their voices ride November's wind. Their thumbprints are on decisions, policies, and laws without which fewer birds would fly wild, fewer wolves would roam free, and fewer fish would swim deep.

These were men and women who took a stand on causes of one kind or another and stepped publicly into the fray. But there are many other, lesser-known mentors who have more quietly shown the way, privately and modestly making a difference through their actions within their own families, communities, or circle of friends. There are also financial supporters, from donors who have provided millions of philanthropic dollars with virtually no fanfare or recognition, to the thousands of individual Canadians who have joined or volunteered for conservation and environmental groups. Also not to be forgotten are those politicians and corporate decision-makers who have had the courage to break ranks and do the right thing, even when it meant going against their peers.

These people, past and present, are Nature's defenders and heroes. Together they form a rough-hewn, but deeply rooted tradition—a legacy of hope and determination for all of us who "cannot live without wild things." It is heartening to remember that we are not alone, but in very fine company.

It's November now, and a late staging loon woke me this morning with a long, lonesome wail. The call of the loon was startling to me, because I had not heard that sound for a month or more, and I would not again for nearly half a year. As the sun rose, I could see the loon's black profile out there, wild and alone in the center of an otherwise ice-bound lake. This summer bird seemed out of place in such a raw wind and bleak backdrop.

Is it really so much to ask, that loons return every year as they always have? Perhaps not, but it is far from assured. Many good souls have helped keep that voice of the wilderness alive so far. Their urgings ride on that voice still, reminding us of what's at stake, cheering us on, and encouraging us when we are losing hope. Our work for Nature is in fact a contract with the past and the future—a pact with our ancestors and our children—to keep the faith for all life on Earth.

Change

FALL IS A SEASON of change. It begins with the yellow-greens of September, it ends with the gray-browns of November, and in between it shows us the riotous orange-reds of October. Fall is both a dénouement for summer and a preparation for winter, the last of the leaves and the first of the snows.

More than any others, two events capture the brooding melancholy of autumn for me. The first is that morning in late September when I search the lake with binoculars from my cabin screened porch, only to find that the two adult loons have left. They were such good company all summer, by day or night, always out there fishing, preening, floating, diving, flapping, and animating a warm, watery world with their laughter and wails. Now the lake gleams quiet, empty of their energy and familiar profiles.

The second is the calling of geese floating high on a prevailing northwesterly wind. The collective tiller of each skein is resolutely set for the South, and the soul of the North is in tow. Up till now, wild tundra grasses have fueled their journey, but tonight the tame corn of farm fields will take over. My heart travels with them.

The Canadian landscape is anchored by two dramatically different seasons from which this book takes its theme: winter and summer (green). If spring builds a bridge between winter and green, then fall is the transition from green to winter. These two dominant moods of Canada in effect need spring and fall as seasonal shoehorns to move gradually from one to the other—from rest (winter), to renewal (spring), to growth (summer), to change (fall). Then the cycle begins again. As with any repeated pattern, we could insert ourselves randomly at any point into the flow, for example, at any day, month, or season, and return a year later to where we began. The length and temperament of Canada's seasons vary from year to year, and each has its own personality, but all four are fundamental to our national psyche. Still, if I had to get stuck in one of them, it would be fall.

Wintergreen — Afterword

ALDO LEOPOLD ORIGINALLY wrote *A Sand County Almanac* under the working title "Great Possessions." Among my greatest "possessions" at Loon Lake are the thick beds of wintergreen plants that carpet the forest floor year-round. Even the phrase "wintergreen" is evocative of the Canadian landscape, seasons, and character. This self-reliant little plant doesn't just endure winter; it relishes it.

With its rich, dark green, leathery leaves and bright red berries, both of which it maintains even under the snow, wintergreen (*Gaultheria procumbens*) is one of Canada's best-known wild plants. A member of the heath family, it has at least twenty-five common or local names. In his 1939 book, *Edible Wild Plants*, Oliver Perry Medsger wrote, "No other wild plant led me into the woods so often as this one. Its mere name recalls many pleasant ramblings afield."

Wintergreen grows three to six inches (7 to 15 cm) high on upright branches from a more extensive system of creeping or underground stems. This invisible interconnected network which supports what we see as an individual plant evokes the complexity of Nature itself and our very limited understanding of it. The less-noticed wintergreen flowers resemble tiny white narrow-mouthed bells nodding singly from the leaf axils; the flower's calyx transforms into the better known cherry-red, berrylike fruit.

Wintergreen is eaten by virtually everything, including small birds, grouse (it is also known as "partridge berry"), ducks, squirrels, deer, bears, and people. The berry's spicy mint flavor is as refreshing as the Canadian north woods themselves. I continually snack on them while hiking, they're quite firm so they don't smash in my pockets, and they can also be used in pies. The aromatic smaller leaves (known as "youngsters") are often chewed directly, and leaves of any age can be brewed into tea (wintergreen is also known as "teaberry"), or refined into the well-known oil of wintergreen. This distinctive flavor is replicated in everything from candy to chewing gum.

As I contemplate a tiny wintergreen plant at the edge of November snow near Loon Lake, I am reminded of William Blake's renowned lines from *Auguries of Innocence*:

> *To see a World in a grain of sand*
> *And a Heaven in a wild flower ...*
> *Keeps the human soul from care.*

Blake's observation stands the test not only of the human imagination, but of modern conservation biology as well, because there is a Heaven to be seen in this wild flower. It is rooted with moss in a bit of shallow glacial till for soil, supporting also a mature stand of white pines, on a granite outcrop jutting into Loon Lake, in the mixed hardwood Great Lakes–St. Lawrence Forest Region, underlain by the parent material of the Canadian Shield, in the eastern part of the North American continent, at 45° 45' latitude and 70° 45' longitude in the Western Hemisphere, of planet Earth, in the solar system orbiting a star we call the Sun, which is moving through the Orion spiral arm of the several-hundred-billion-star Milky Way galaxy, which is part of the Local Group of galaxies, knotted together into a larger supercluster of at least 5,000 galaxies, of which "at least fifty billion" are currently thought to make up the Universe. The beautiful small wintergreen (itself made up of tissues, cells, molecules, atoms, protons, neutrons, quarks, electrons, neutrinos, and leptons) can exist only because it is nested in, and nourished by, an expanding series of interacting ecological envelopes, which quite literally give it life.

In 1981, when we founded the Canadian Council on Ecological Areas, ecologist Stan Rowe quipped that we should really have called it the Canadian Council on Ecological *Volumes*. This, he argued, would encourage humans to think of ecosystems three-dimensionally or volumetrically, and as being nested within each other like Russian dolls. Blake, therefore, could just as well have observed that we can "See a wild flower in a Heaven," but to do this we would have to begin from a different vantage point—with the largest Russian doll (the Universe) and think inward. Again, each ecological envelope forms the context and is a precondition for the next, peeling each back until we reach the tiny inner doll (the wildflower).

The image conjured up resembles nested segments of a magnificent "telescope of being" whose full expansiveness can be appreciated by peering in from either end, smaller to larger or larger to smaller, depending on where the viewer is located. By design or by chance, we humans were located somewhere toward the small end of the great telescope of being, here on Earth. It is therefore from *this* place that we can glimpse and marvel at things larger and smaller that form the life-giving context for wintergreen and people alike.

At the age of seven I first experienced Canada from the air, flying Trans-Canada Airlines (in an old prop-driven North Star) from Ontario to visit my grandparents' farm in Saskatchewan. I remember staring fascinated, nonstop, out the window at the natural quilt of my country—the lakes, rivers, forests, and fields. At night, only the occasional twinkling light portrayed the lives of Canadians embedded in the landscape below. Later, in 1958, I "ground-truthed" much the same journey by bus, out of the north woods, across the prairies, and into the foothills to Banff when that town was still a rustic little mountain community. These were deeply formative experiences for me.

Today my work takes me back and forth across Canada perhaps twenty times a year. Still, my eye is held captive by the beauty gliding by that airplane window. Still, when I'm returning over the Atlantic my heart bumps when the first glimpse of home is the wild coast of Labrador—such a contrast to the entirely civilized land I last touched in Europe. And I can only imagine the likes of astronaut Roberta Bondar, "coming home to Canada" again and again as she orbited the Earth. That experience also left her firmly committed to conserving the bits of wild fabric we still have in this part of the world. As Canadians and all citizens of the world move into the first century of a new millennium, we must decide what role we want wilderness to play in our lives and what provision we are prepared to make for it. We are likely the last generation to have any choice in the matter.

Ironically, it is technology, which we have traditionally used to devastate so much of the Earth, that may now help us to save it. Technology linked with wisdom, that is.

Through humans traveling by airplane or spacecraft, or through technological extensions of humanity such as the Hubble telescope, we have a profound opportunity to situate ourselves. When afforded that opportunity, we have indeed marveled at what we saw, when looking further out, for example, to see stars or galaxies in virtually every direction, as in the now famous "Hubble Deep Field" poster, or when looking back on our own blue home planet. At moments like this, we are reminded that "ecology" is derived from the Greek word *oikos*, which means "home."

When a humble wintergreen plant, my modest cabin on Loon Lake, our species, and our Earth are perceived and understood in this broader context, it gives deeper meaning to the nature of Life itself—a wonderful gift from all that permeates and surrounds. In his collection of essays on ecology called *Home Place*, Rowe shows us that Life is a property vested not in individual organisms, but in the "global environment (the ecosphere) from which all evolved and by which all are sustained."

It follows that, to save Life on Earth, we must save the very preconditions for Life. Therefore, saving species means saving places, means saving the Life-giving ecological processes that make species and places possible. And the processes that sustain us can be understood as extending well beyond our Earthly ecosphere, to the realms that make our ecosphere possible, namely, the star nurseries wherein planets, suns, and galaxies themselves are still being born.

For now, there's not much we can do to conserve star nurseries. But the Earth's ecosphere is another matter. Step one is realizing that this is what we are truly trying to save.

To aid my own understanding of what's at stake, I find
another image helpful, borrowed from Newfoundland and
Labrador wildlife biologist Dennis Minty. Think of our
planet as an apple. In cross-section, the apple has a large
inner white part and a thin outer skin. These are analogous
to the Earth's abiotic core, and the thin sensitive ecosphere
wherein exists all life as we know it. The ecosphere is in fact
a phase boundary, the point of interface between land, oceans,
and air. You and I are positioned and existing right now in
this phase boundary. We could not exist without it. Along
with all other living things, we reside here in the skin of the
apple, here in a vital, breathing membrane—a blue-green
film of Life energized by the Sun.

Earth's continents, oceans, and biomes such as forests,
deserts, mountains, and grasslands are like curved jigsaw
pieces that fit together to form the round enveloping
ecosphere. So words like "mosaic" and "quilt," just like the
image of seeing a Heaven in a wild flower, are more than
compelling poetry. They are also very good biology. And the
species that tend to interest naturalists so much—fascinating
creations like birds, animals, and wintergreen wildflowers
—are almost imperceptible specks inhabiting these puzzle
pieces that make up the apple's skin. The specks are entirely
the products of, and nourished by, the living ecosphere.
Conversely, if we lose or impair a critical number of the
specks, we endanger the larger puzzle pieces, and by
extension the entire ecosphere.

Like an apple's skin, some parts of the Earth's ecosphere
have been severely bruised or scarred. The top and bottom
of the Earth-apple's skin, for example, are experiencing

serious tears though holes in the ozone layer. These tears may be causing dramatic declines in some of the specks worldwide, species like reptiles and amphibians. And entire areas of the apple's skin-surface are being degraded by pollution, especially the oceans, or by deforestation or desertification in the case of the land components.

The point is that it is not just the species-specks that we are now in danger of losing. We are jeopardizing the membrane itself—our life-support system. If we focus all our attention on the specks, rather than saving the life-conveying skin, we are in danger of fiddling while Rome burns. What's at stake is the crucible of Life itself—the evolutionary potential of our planet. Understood in this way, the true scale of modern conservation becomes clear, which in turn helps us set meaningful benchmarks for success.

Now, do all of these metaphors—ecological envelopes, nesting Russian dolls, the great telescope of being, and some ecospheric skin of the apple—really flood over me simply at the sight of a tiny wintergreen plant? Frankly, yes, because this is what *all* living things bring to mind. Obviously, something other than wintergreen could equally serve as the medium or "wildflower" through which we all can "see a Heaven," in Blake's words. And no doubt there are other metaphors or images that could help us to better understand the nature of Nature. But a transformation of that understanding is deeply needed if we are to avoid squandering the wild flowers Heaven has given us.

In practical terms, of course, natural delights such as wildflowers and wintergreen are not anyone's "possessions" at all, even on private land. Because land ownership does not make these things "mine," so much as it allows me to influence what happens to them. And that influence can be exercised responsibly, or not. Leopold's guidance on this matter was: "A thing is right when it tends to preserve the integrity, stability and beauty of the biotic community. It is wrong when it tends otherwise."

These are the perspectives and core values that must drive a land ethic, not just for Loon Lake, but for our country, and our planet. Without such an ethic, all other human strivings will amount to little, or nothing.

Appendix

CONSERVATION AGREEMENTS

Terms like *conservation agreement, easement,* and *covenant* are often used interchangeably. Although these concepts may sound complicated, it is important to understand that what they accomplish is really quite simple: *all of them help you legally restrict what happens to your land for as long as you wish.*

Here is what I did for Loon Lake. First, I sat down at the table in my cabin with a blank sheet of paper in front of me to reflect on why this property was important to me. What was it about Loon Lake that I valued? In a few words, and in plain language, I wrote down answers to these questions as best I could. Second, I wrote down what should *not* happen to Loon Lake, both now and after I'm gone, in order to protect the things I value about it. The things I didn't want to see happen became my "restrictions."

There is no predetermined or expected set of goals and restrictions required for a conservation agreement; the list is entirely up to you. Once you are this far into the process, you will have already done the most important thinking, which, if you wish, can form the basis of a legal document.

The next step is to contact the Nature Conservancy of Canada or any one of the hundreds of other groups authorized to execute conservation agreements in Canada (this list can be obtained from the Nature Conservancy or the federal government's Canadian Wildlife Service). The conservation group you choose will help you translate your plain-language restrictions into legal terms that can be binding for as long as you want.

These restrictions are then registered on title, so that any future landowner will be advised of them and bound by them. Of course you must agree to abide by your own restrictions, and you sign an agreement with your conservation group promising to do so. This group is responsible for ensuring that your restrictions are respected, now and into the future, with specified penalties to set things right if they aren't. Nevertheless, you retain complete private ownership of your property. If for some reason the group monitoring your easement is unable to do so, for example if it winds down, it is responsible for finding another group to carry on.

Now—as if ensuring that the place you love will be protected in perpetuity weren't enough—there can also be some very attractive financial benefits to a conservation agreement. Since you have legally restricted the use of your property, you are judged to have reduced its resale value in current real estate terms. Therefore, an independent appraiser can determine what your land was worth *before* your conservation restrictions went into effect (say, $75,000), versus what your land is worth *after* you have restricted its use (say, $50,000). The *difference* (in this case, $25,000) is deemed to be the *value* of your conservation agreement, which can be donated to the conservation group you are dealing with. They, in turn, will issue you a $25,000 charitable receipt, which you can use in the normal fashion as a tax credit toward your federal income tax! Revenue Canada now regards the donation of conservation agreements as "ecological gifts."

Finally, let's say you don't own land now, but you would *like* to for the purpose of protection. The problem is figuring out how to afford it. Well, conservation agreements in effect provide a mechanism to obtain a significant cash refund, in the form of a charitable tax deduction, which you could use to offset some of the purchase price of your property after you buy it. The Nature Conservancy of Canada maintains a list of priority properties they would love to have someone purchase on just this basis.

It is not possible for me to anticipate or cover in depth all the details regarding conservation agreements in a short appendix. But if the basic idea interests you, why not contact the Nature Conservancy or your local land trust or naturalist group to see how this concept might work for you? It makes a wonderful gift for the ecological future of your country, and serves as an effective way to extend stewardship of a place you love, beyond your lifetime. Although future generations could well hold us responsible for having protected too little, they are unlikely to blame anyone for having protected too much of Canada.

References

Banfield, A.W. F. 1974. *The Mammals of Canada*. Toronto: University of Toronto Press.

Dickinson, Terence. 1983. *Nightwatch*. Revised (with extensive updating) and reprinted 1989. Toronto: Firefly Books.

Dunning, Joan. 1985. *The Loon: Voice of the Wilderness*. Dublin, New Hampshire: Yankee Publishing.

Godfrey, W. Earl. 1986. *The Birds of Canada*, Revised edition. Ottawa: National Museums of Canada.

Leopold, Aldo. 1949. *A Sand County Almanac*. New York: Oxford University Press.

Medsger, Oliver Perry. 1939. *Edible Wild Plants*. New York: Macmillan.

Mitchell, W.O. 1947. *Who Has Seen the Wind?* Toronto: Macmillan of Canada.

Murie, Olaus J. 1954. *A Field Guide to Animal Tracks*. Boston: Houghton Mifflin.

National Audubon Society. 1988. *Pocket Guide: Insects and Spiders*. New York: Alfred A. Knopf.

Olson, Sigurd F. 1958. *Listening Point*. New York: Alfred A. Knopf.

Pruitt, William O., Jr. 1960. *Wild Harmony: Animals of the North*. Vancouver: Douglas and McIntyre.

Rezendes, Paul. 1992. *Tracking and the Art of Seeing*. Charlotte, Vermont: Camden House.

Rowe, Stan. 1990. *Home Place*. Edmonton: NeWest Publishers Limited.

Standing Senate Committee on Agriculture, Fisheries and Forestry Commission and Private Legislation Branch. 1984. *Soil at Risk: Canada's Eroding Future*. Ottawa: Senate of Canada.

About the Author

MONTE HUMMEL WAS born in the fall of 1946 in, of all places, downtown Toronto. As a young boy, he moved 1900 km northwest to Whitedog Falls, where his father worked in a hydro camp in the bush north of Kenora, Ontario. There, Monte fell in love with the woods, hiking, building log forts, and informally guiding fishermen on the English River to earn pocket money. Ten years after leaving, he revisited his home river to discover it had been contaminated with mercury, leaving the Ojibway community there in social and economic despair. This personal experience led directly to a lifelong career of environmental advocacy.

In the late fifties, Monte moved back South to attend high school (Ancaster), followed by university (Toronto) where he won the E.J. Sanford Gold Medal in Philosophy and earned a B.A. (1969), M.A. in Philosophy (1970), and an M.Sc. in Forestry (1979). He worked his way through school as a wilderness canoe tripping guide.

In 1969, Monte co-founded Pollution Probe, of which he became Executive Director, and later Chairman. Between 1977 and 1982, he also coordinated the undergraduate program in Environmental Studies at the University of Toronto. And in 1978, he joined World Wildlife Fund Canada as Executive Director, becoming President in 1985, the position he still holds. He has served on the boards of more than thirty Canadian and international conservation organizations, been appointed to numerous government advisory councils, testified before various parliamentary committees, and is Past President of the Labrador Retriever Club of Ontario.

A well-known public speaker, Monte Hummel is author of more than one hundred popular articles and scientific journal publications, a contributor to many books, and author or editor of four previous books: *Arctic Wildlife* (1984), *Endangered Spaces* (1989), *Wild Hunters* (co-authored with his wife, Sherry Pettigrew, 1991), and *Protecting Canada's Endangered Spaces* (1995).

Monte maintains a demanding work schedule persuading senior decision-makers to protect wild places, and travels to all parts of the Canadian landscape, which he loves and defends fiercely. He has two grown children, Robin and Doug, and when he is not on the road, at his desk, or hiking and canoeing from his cabin at Loon Lake, he lives quietly in the country with Sherry near the small town of Beeton, Ontario.